Shared reading
in practice

RETHINKING READING

Series Editor: L. John Chapman
School of Education, The Open University

Shared reading in practice

CHRIS DAVIS AND
ROSEMARY STUBBS

Open University Press
Milton Keynes • *Philadelphia*

Open University Press
Open University Educational Enterprises Limited
12 Cofferidge Close
Stony Stratford
Milton Keynes MK11 1BY

and

242 Cherry Street
Philadelphia, PA 19106, USA

First Published 1988

British Library Cataloguing in Publication Data

Davis, Chris.
  Shared reading in practice.
  1. Reading. Learning by children.
  Psychological aspects
  I. Title   II. Stubbs, Rosemary
  428.4'01'9

  ISBN 0-335-09510-0
  ISBN 0-335-09509-7 Pbk

Library of Congress Cataloging-in-Publication Data

Davis, Chris.
  Shared reading in practice/Chris Davis, Rosemary Stubbs.
  p.   cm.
  Bibliography: p.
  Includes index.
  ISBN 0-335-09510-0   ISBN 0-335-09509-7 (pbk.)
  1. Reading--Great Britain--Parent participation--Case studies.
2. Home and school--Great Britain--Case studies.   I. Stubbs, Rosemary. II. Title
LB1050.2.D38 1988   88-22408
372.4--dc19   CIP

Typeset by Burns & Smith, Derby
Printed in Great Britain by the Alden Press, Oxford

Contents

Foreword

In reviewing research on reading in 1977 Moseley and Moseley concluded from the evidence then available that children's reading and language performance benefits when 'home and school support each other in progress towards mutually understood and agreed goals'. Since that date further evidence has proliferated (Tizard *et al*. 1982, Topping and Wolfendale 1985 and Swinson 1986) and there are shared reading and parental involvement projects all over the country.

The purpose of this book is to provide practical advice on introducing shared reading to children, parents and colleagues in a positive and constructive manner. Such an approach is not easy, but rests essentially on mutual trust, agreement and understanding. This foreword is an attempt to explain why shared reading is successful and why it is spreading so quickly at this particular time. I would suggest that it is because, as an approach, it is consonant with our increased awareness and understanding of the development of children's language and learning, and also with our understanding of the nature of literacy.

It is interesting to note how technological advances have facilitated such awareness. For example, early attempts to program computers to use language highlighted the complexity of language and provided a new perspective on the language learning task that many children have almost accomplished by the time they come into school. From Ruth Weir's (1962) tape recordings of her son's language play before he fell asleep at night it became clear that children do not extend their language by the simple repetition of adults' words. Her son was extending and creating his language by responding to the patterns of sound and structure of which he was aware and was experimenting with these. Earlier work on language development based on increase in vocabulary alone (Templin 1957) was superseded by studies of children's language development in their own homes, using tape recorders, radio microphones, film and videotape (Brown and Bellugi 1964, Trevarthen 1974, Halliday 1975 and Wells 1982).

As a result of this, attention shifted from the study of small units of language to the study of sequences of discourse (Wells 1982, Blank *et al*. 1978) and whole texts. Linked to this was the acceptance that language develops through interaction with someone else, when both participants are attending to and share an interest in the same subject or object. A central concern of these studies was the role of parents and other adults in children's development (Tizard *et al.* 1980). Following a similar path, psychologists concerned with the development of children's thinking (Donaldson 1978, Donaldson *et al.* 1983) moved towards studying children in more naturalistic settings and in doing so noted the benefits of children working together on problems.

For teachers this has led to an increased awareness of the learning and kinds of knowing that children bring with them when they come to school (Paley 1981). It has also encouraged an increase in collaborative learning activities between children and between adults. At the same time there has been an increasing awareness of the nature of literacy and its development before school. It is now clear that most children come to school with a developing concept of story (Applebee 1978), with a sense that the language of books is different from everyday language (Clark 1976). Children in our society do not meet print for the first time when they enter school; they grow up surrounded by print in shops, on labels and on television and they have their own ideas about how it works (Clay 1972, Ferreiro 1985, Goodman 1984).

Even at secondary school level, group reading and discussion activities have proved a powerful means of learning (Davies and Greene 1984) and as Lunzer and Gardner (1979) discovered:

> learning is enhanced when more than one language mode is employed... When they are used together in the same setting, reading may provide the stimulus to thinking; spoken language gives it reality and sustains it; finally, writing crystallizes the product.

Shared reading fits into this overall pattern by contributing to the continuity of experience for the child from home to school. It is about sharing complete meaningful texts, whether story or information. In the sharing the gap may be bridged between spoken and written language because there is a voice to listen to and a face to look at. Gradually the child is able to take on the rhythms and patterns of continuous written texts without losing the sense of what is being read, and at the same time builds up expectations and predictions about different types of text. Such is the basis of fluent reading. Sharing a book continues the process of language development that started at birth. Sharing a book allows opportunities to talk about writing and language itself (Cazden 1983). It allows consideration of style and of the person who wrote the book (Anderson 1983). In our increasingly complex society we require adults and children who not only read the written word but who question it. Sharing a book allows for mismatches or misunderstandings of, for example, social or cultural setting (Steffensen 1981, Anderson 1984) to be made explicit.

The obvious extension of shared reading then is shared writing. Such an approach relies heavily on parents', teachers' and librarians' knowledge of books. There are increasing numbers of excellent books being produced and only detailed knowledge of these will enable adults to support and monitor the continuing development of children's facility with written language throughout all of the school years.

Eleanor Anderson B.A; M.Phil.
Senior Lecturer, Hatfield Polytechnic School of Education.

Acknowledgements

We are grateful to the County Education Officer, Chief Adviser, teachers, parents and children in Hertfordshire who gave us the opportunity to develop our ideas on reading.

Introduction

This book has been written in response to many teachers' requests that we record our experiences and observations made during our own journey along the path towards shared reading.

Chris, having entered teaching as a mature student, found that parental involvement was part of her reception class approach to learning. As a mother she had been actively involved in the pre-school playgroup movement, so to her it was quite natural to continue to use parent expertise. In the small all-white school it is very much part of the focus of the school as a central part of community life.

In contrast, Rosemary teaches in a large urban infant school where 30 per cent of the children are Asian in origin. She returned to teaching three years ago to a large class which contained a sizeable group of summer-born middle infants. She began involving parents with their children's reading as an attempt to make up the difference that the two years only of Infant education would make.

Over the past few years more and more schools have been exploring and developing areas of the curriculum where parental help may be beneficial. Obviously it is in the early years of education, where there are closer home/school links, that teachers find more opportunities to involve parents. Now, however, there is increasing evidence of many imaginative schemes encouraging parent participation right through to sixth form level. It could be argued that if parents are accepted as equal partners in the beginning stages of learning, then this support should be continued and valued throughout the child's school career. Unfortunately, with many children passing through at least four schools during their compulsory years of education, it is unlikely that they will encounter a common attitude to parental involvement in all those schools. Such parental involvement has, by law, become part of our schools' management system and in 1988 parent governors will be becoming much more influential on our governing bodies. It is in the interest of all schools, therefore, to ensure that such parents act positively and constructively for the good of the schools and its pupils. The only ways of achieving this are by effective channels of communication and by the encouragement of active parent participation in the classroom.

Most nursery and infant teachers use parental assistance in some learning activities. As long ago as 1964 Douglas concluded that children with poor home support were less successful in school. Research carried out in Haringey (Tizard *et al.* 1982) and Sheffield (Ashton *et al.* 1986) continued to demonstrate the advantages of parental help. Involvement in the teaching of reading is the obvious area to start with and when this has been monitored the increased success in reading has been observed.

Since then, however, our approach to children's reading has begun to change. Both teachers and children have become dissatisfied with the stilted, restricted language of reading scheme material. Observation shows that learning to read need not involve daily reading of two or three pages and a progressive advance through structured levels of vocabulary. Children's enthusiasm and success in reading is being achieved through reading whole stories of their choice at a sitting, with support from another 'reader' (child or adult). Parents are now getting satisfaction from the mutual enjoyment of a wide range of good literature. Teachers are still supervising reading material, implementing language programmes, monitoring individual progression and, at the same time, reaping the benefits of a partnership with parents, but, above all, children are benefiting from this additional one-to-one attention and are now reflecting this early exposure to a wider vocabulary in their writing and in their oral communication.

CHAPTER 1

Why involve the parents?

What a transformation there is in the attitude of a five-year-old today, compared with, say, 1968. Twenty years ago teachers emerged from college, eager to begin putting all their theory into practice in their first reception class, and were faced with 40 subdued, apprehensive, often tearful children. Mothers were expected only to deposit their offspring at the threshold of the classroom, exchange a few words with teacher and disappear until 3.30 p.m. Today, thank goodness, most five-year-olds will have made one or more visits to their new class, will probably have attended a playgroup or nursery and will gradually be assimilated into school, with a parent supporting them, if necessary. In practice, parental presence at this stage is usually superfluous or short-term, since most children arrive at school already eager to learn, confident and self-reliant. Several reasons could be suggested for this perceived modification in child behaviour:

1. A succession of experts on child care has increasingly advocated a more 'child-centred' approach to family life.
2. Comprehensive pre-school monitoring by health visitors and clinics has led to the identification of physical, emotional and behavioural problems at an early stage.
3. Increased stimulation from birth, with activity toys, mothers and toddlers groups, etc. has produced a generation of children who are familiar with a variety of purposeful activities and play experiences.
4. Television, in particular, has increased the children's general knowledge and awareness of wider horizons.
5. Increased interaction with parents and other adults has led to an ability to communicate well, and in most cases to a fluent and confident use of language.

Obviously this does not apply to all children starting school, but in fact the gap is now widening between those children who have benefited from all these pre-school influences, and those who have not been exposed to such factors for one reason or another. The reasons for the poor performance of some children have been well researched and documented, and influences such as home background, ethnic origins, position in family and familial relationships are indisputable factors. We need to look at the positive side and ask, 'What common factor is producing our current generation of healthy, alert, well-adjusted, sociable five-year-olds?' and 'How can we maintain these attitudes throughout adolescence and into adulthood?' It is fascinating to discover that in her small-scale study of young fluent readers in Scotland (1976), Clark found that the common factors among these 32 children were:

1. All the mothers were over 20 at the time of these children's birth (15 of them over 30) and that they 'all expressed interest in their child's progress and found the children stimulating companions'.
2. Few of the mothers had worked while the children were of pre-school age, and only six of the children had attended nursery school. Thus Clark suggests that a child who starts school already reading fluently is likely to have had a great deal of home-based stimulation from mature, concerned adults.

In other words these children arrive at school a product of, in most cases, one or more secure, loving relationships. Developing within the framework of these relationships, the pre-school child has already acquired many skills, most of which are included in the list drawn up by Young and Tyre (1986).

What parents traditionally teach in 60 months

- Crawling, standing, walking, running, jumping, climbing and going up and down stairs.
- Eating using knife, fork and spoon.
- Drinking from cup or glass.
- Dressing, tying knots, use of buttons and zips.
- Washing, bathing, cleaning teeth.
- Toilet training by day and night.
- Skipping, hopping, skating and cycling (but not 'traffic safe')
- Swimming in learner pool.
- Playing alone, with other children and adults, taking turns and learning the rules.
- To know own name, sex, age, birthday, address and way round neighbourhood ('not traffic safe').
- To use pencils, crayons, paints to draw people, houses, common objects; circles, squares, lines, triangles (but not a diamond).
- To count to about 20, know fingers on each hand (5 + 5 + 10), recognize digits, repeat numbers like 47582.
- To cut out common shapes with scissors, cut things in halves, make models in 3D.
- To behave appropriately with family, relatives, friends, strangers, in a variety of social settings.
- To talk and to understand language using the complete grammatical system correctly; to ask and answer questions; to follow and to give instructions; to follow and to tell stories; to describe, compare and contrast; to define things by their use;

to know names of days, months, seasons, colours, coins; to use language in social relationships and to guide actions; to use about 2000 words.

- To enjoy being read to and to have begun to read – some to read fluently, some only recognizing odd words and letters.
- To write own name and most letters of the alphabet – some to write messages, some to enjoy copying.
- To care for younger children, for pets, performing useful tasks about the house and garden with minimum supervision.

(Young and Tyre 1986)

Much of this teaching will have been carried out by caring parents or substitute parents, themselves gaining great enjoyment and satisfaction from watching the child gradually mastering each skill. Most of these skills are acquired simply by the child observing others and imitating them naturally and spontaneously, with plenty of practice, encouragement and support. Think, for example, of all the stages of learning to walk, all achieved eventually but at a different pace, in a different way, at a different age according to the individual child. Parents are responsible for the competent teaching of walking and all these other skills because they know their children so intimately that they can sense exactly what to do and how and when to do it. So, when parents have been so closely and successfully involved in their children's pre-school learning, surely it is unrealistic to expect them to suddenly back off and hand over the teaching entirely to schools?

Certainly teachers have been trained in classroom management, curriculum planning, child psychology and development, and have a wide knowledge of their specialist subject areas. But with large classes it is extremely difficult for a teacher to build up and maintain the same one-to-one adult/child relationship which has produced this rapid pre-school acquisition of skills. We believe that by involving parents particularly in the first years of schooling, children will benefit by naturally developing their pre-school skills into the areas of reading, writing and numeracy. This approach offers more opportunities for practising these skills and, even more important, the chance to maintain the child/adult interaction so conducive to a good pattern of language development. 'Parents know more about their own children and the knowledge they have than teachers do. So the relationship has to be a true partnership and a sharing of knowledge and expertise rather than a semi-apprenticeship relationship set up by most schools' (Smidt 1986).

Parental involvement has been identified by some as the greatest development in education since the setting up of compulsory state education. A succession of government reports has led to a gradual increase in home/school initiatives. Plowden (1967) stated that parental attitudes could be influenced by improved communication and information from the school. Then in 1975, Bullock recommended that not only were good communication skills important in the early stages of learning, but that parents had their part to play in this process. 'There is, then, no doubt whatever of the value of parents' involvement in the early stages of reading. What needs careful thought is the nature of that involvement and the attitude they bring to it.' The Taylor Report (1977) really developed the whole idea of parents as equal partners, emphasizing that teachers are linked to parents by the children for whom they are both responsible. 'Every parent has a right to expect a school's teachers to recognize his status in the education of his child, by the practical arrangements they make to communicate with him and the spirit in which they accept his interest.' So although by this stage parents have already been involved in many school activities – through PTAs, helping in the classroom and as members of the governing body – parental partnership is now developing into a more open relationship between home and school.

Once the aura of mystique, particularly about the teaching of reading, has been removed, our experience suggests that almost all parents want to be involved in their own children's education. Some may hold back, initially, either because they are unfamiliar with modern practice or maybe have negative feelings about schools themselves. These fears may be allayed by giving parents plenty of opportunities to watch their children learning and to observe their interaction with other children, parents or teachers. Midwinter (1972) observed,

> the crucial need is for parents to understand their children's education and this is particularly true in areas where parents have not always enjoyed educational success themselves, and have not had much opportunity to study modern methods. To understand they must see and hear what is going on – the logic of it is to see, understand and support.

So this approach to learning is based on the belief that a child's personality, motivation and attitude are gradually formed by the kinds of relationships he makes with those people who are important to him. These vital relationships begin at birth and are vitally important at the pre-school and primary stage, when children learn happily and confidently with a relaxed, positive approach. Children acquire new skills not only because it gives pleasure and satisfaction to their parents, but because they themselves are made to feel it is a worthwhile activity, bringing praise and success. If we, as teachers, can emulate this parental behaviour, then ideally the partnership between parents and teachers can only enhance the child's whole educational experience. Our observations in Chapter 5 echo the proposals of Wood (1974) in his study on 'Parents and the Curriculum', These were that:

1. School performance of children whose parents were drawn into the curriculum improves more than those whose parents are not involved.
2. Responsiveness of parents is independent of their child's academic status and of parental social class.
3. A high degree of parental involvement in the curriculum is associated with a favourable change in the attitudes of parents to school and education generally.
4. School performance of children whose parents become more favourable improve more than those children with parents whose attitudes remain static or regress.

Better Schools (DES 1985) advocates that many more schools should take a wider view of how parents can be involved in education, both at home and in the classroom. The most natural area to begin with is the early stages of language and reading development, using the skills that the parents have already put to use in the home.

'I do and I understand'

CHAPTER 2

The role of the parent

The role of the parent very much depends on the attitude of the teacher, and the nature of the task allotted to the parent. Wood (1974) maintains that there are four levels of parental involvement. At the first level, the parent's role is purely observational, confined to attending open days or concerts. The second stage is instructional, with the parent working alongside the teacher in the classroom. The third level is practical, with parents more involved in children's learning, attending educational meetings etc. The fourth level Wood describes is formal where parents are involved in planning of the school curriculum and acting as parent govenors. Obviously to reach the fourth formal stage of commitment, schools and parents ideally would have experienced a lengthy period of working together through the first three stages, so building up a real sense of mutual trust and true partnership. We would actually re-order the stages of Wood's levels of involvement: OBSERVATIONAL; PRACTICAL; INSTRUCTIONAL; FORMAL.

In some areas such as Coventry the introduction of parental involvement has been facilitated by the appointment of community advisers and teachers responsible for home/school liaison. In the main, however, the individual ethos of each school dictates the roles taken by parents.

Since the reduction in the number of welfare helpers, there are few primary school teachers who refuse any offer of 'a spare pair of hands'. And even while performing some menial task, such as washing paintpots or helping a child dress after PE, that 'extra pair of hands' belongs to an interested adult, who can relate to the children as required – as helper, comforter, listener, parent. There are so many needs to be met by the primary teacher, at any one time, that regular parent volunteers to assist generally are invaluable and this role is a vital one.

The role of instructor is equally important. Again the opportunity for a group of children or maybe an individual to have the undivided attention of one adult is so necessary for effective learning. However well organized the class teacher may be, however independently the children may learn, large class sizes and an ever-widening curriculum result in few opportunities for uninterrupted, prolonged, meaningful child/teacher interaction. An extra adult to delegate to this type of role is welcome, whether it is to discuss a picture with a child needing stimulus for language development, or to provide practical help for a child measuring the playground. It is at this level that parents can provide so much support and time for reading, enjoying books together at all levels of ability. How rewarding it is to sit down and enjoy a whole story, with time to discuss the illustrations or characters, with the child involving himself in the book. The parents themselves, with a little training, enjoy the satisfaction of seeing how children learn so easily, given the extra practice and stimulation they can provide. At the same time, as parents absorb the atmosphere of the classroom, our experience shows that the majority quickly come to an understanding of the way children learn, and an appreciation of the conditions needed to provide a stimulating learning environment.

As parents become more familiar with the school environment, so their interest in education generally may increase. Some may be interested in borrowing books to back-up their activities in the classroom or the home (see booklist of parents on page 80). Others will enjoy the stimulation of meetings on different aspects of the curriculum, with talks by teachers, visiting speakers or maybe relevant videos. We attended a parent evening recently where we gave an introductory presentation on shared reading, after which parents divided up into small discussion groups. Each group appointed a 'scribe' who noted the issues discussed and questions raised. A final session involved a general airing of these items, with debate continuing until almost midnight! There were some areas of uncertainty and disagreement, but how much more positive for such thoughts to be openly discussed in a relaxed atmosphere, than for parents to niggle away in the background. Such occasions are not for all parents, however, and we are aware of the problem of involving those parents we never see.

To return to Wood's levels of parent involvement, there is no doubt that all schools would be delighted if they could get every parent to function at the basic observational level. Even this role is crucial with so much evidence to show how children's learning is influenced by parental interest and encouragement. 'The major influence on a child's ability to take advantage of educational opportunity seems to be his parents' attitudes to education and their interest in his school work' (Douglas 1964). In primary schools, where concerts and plays tend to involve the whole school, the majority of children usually get some parental support at this level. This role is more difficult to achieve at secondary school where the children often get involved in such activities on a voluntary basis. In many schools the observational role is being offered to parents increasingly in other ways. Classroom open days are becoming common practice, where parents can spend time watching their child taking part in a range of learning activities. These are happily possible in the secondary as well as the primary sector, though obviously less inhibited in the latter.

Another excellent way of involving parents in school is to organize a workshop. One local school plans such a workshop each year, based on a particular curricular area – maths, literacy, etc. or possibly on a topic which is cross-curricular (e.g. colour). The staff each make themselves responsible for particular areas of the workshop, which in this instance is set up for about two weeks around the school hall, allowing plenty of space for a variety of activities. Then each class is timetabled for specific sessions in the workshop, giving children access to a variety of learning experiences not always readily available in the classroom. For instance, an animal theme produced an area housing all the current school pets – placed there for practical sessions of observation, comparison, etc. At the same time, parents are invited to come in for hour sessions to help children with workshop activities. Also, every parent is given the opportunity to observe their child's class using the workshop.

'Put it away, Cynthia!'

It is a good idea to hold one or more of these open sessions in the evening, as there are obviously so many parents who find it difficult to take time off from work. One local secondary school closes for its afternoon session, and then transfers the whole afternoon timetable to the evening. Some parents still need plenty of encouragement even to adopt the observer role, but time and concentration on this area are never wasted, since it is only after participation at this level that some parents may want to commit themselves further. There is no doubt that many parents themselves have unhappy memories of school, and ice-breaking activities can sometimes work wonders in producing a more positive attitude. A teacher at one school put up paper and the vaguest outline for a large mural. All parents attending an open evening were invited to add to it. Some added a large proportion displaying considerable artistic talent; others added a small corner, but what fun for parents and children to admire the end product – vivid and spectacular! As a direct result, two or three parents agreed to come in and help the children in art lessons, and lend a hand with scenery painting.

Another group of parents who will often need a more individual approach are some of ethnic minority origin. In this instance, we must examine the reasons for some parents' reluctance to come to school. The obvious one may be a poor command of English and we must be prepared to overcome this problem by the provision of letters home in mother tongue, by using interpreters at parent evenings, and by more home visiting. Some of these parents may have a background of isolation from the school, with no previous experience of school/parent co-operation. There may be a case for holding a separate initial meeting for such parents, if numbers demand it, where they may feel less threatened by the British education system, so often seen by many as supported by white middle-class parents. If teachers make a determined effort to involve EVERY parent, these attitudes could slowly be modified. We visited a Hertfordshire school recently where the pupils were 50 per cent Bengali. Many of the parents lived some distance from the school and had younger children at home. This particular school had initiated a number of approaches, aimed at first at the mothers. Many attended a weekly 'mother and toddler' group in the school hall; others had begun to attend neighbourhood English classes; health visitors and teachers were working together, talking to small groups of women in one of their homes. This was an excellent opportunity to discuss such matters as basic child care, local amenities and school activities.

In many North Hertfordshire schools, with a longer-established ethnic minority population, parents are making a real contribution to raising the self-esteem of black children, by involving themselves in the running of schools and sharing their own talents in the classroom – in one case sharing mother tongue folk stories regularly, and in another case organizing lessons in traditional Indian dancing (this is very popular and open to all – children and teachers, black and white).

Having found some means of involving all parents as OBSERVERS, it is to be hoped that more will feel able to be involved on the PRACTICAL level. In addition there are some parents who prefer to take on the role of INSTRUCTOR where they can really feel part of the learning process in school.

It is only the minority of parents who will actually have the time and the inclination to involve themselves on a FORMAL basis and obviously this group will include parent governors and others really interested in the school organization and curriculum development. It is to be hoped that any parent wanting to contribute in this way will be given every opportunity to do so. In some schools parent groups meet regularly, not necessarily as PTAs engaged in fund-raising (that has to be classified as a practical role!), but as groups interested in discussing different aspects of education. In one local village school, each governor has taken responsibility for finding out about one curriculum area, spending some time in school observing and then reporting back.

Clearly this increase in parental awareness and involvement is all part of the 1980s trend towards a more consumer-orientated society, and very much linked with an awareness of individual rights. A more open and accessible education system must be welcomed by parents and teachers. What must not be lost, however, is the professionalism of teachers, and it is in the handling of the parent/teacher roles that experience and training are required. Schools must allow individual teachers to involve parents, to whatever extent the teacher wishes. Some teachers may prefer no participation, others may extend it to all areas of the curriculum.

Having made the decision to welcome parents into the classroom, then each teacher should initially define their view of the child/parent/teacher relationship, which will probably cover some of the following points:

1. Parents must accept that there is an element of confidentiality (i.e. they must not reveal the abilities or behaviour problems of individual children to all and sundry).
2. Parents are taken on as partners, aware that the class teacher has the managerial oversight of the whole class. Teacher and parent each have an expertise to give to the children. But it is on the teacher that overall responsibility rests and in no way is any of this responsibility diminished.
3. The teacher has established a framework for class organization and discipline, based on training and experience in assessing the needs of the group and of individual children.

If parents are volunteering to participate in schools for the right reasons, then these constraints are assumed, and caring parents will continue to trust in the professional expertise of the majority of teachers. These are the parents who, we hope, could follow the recommendations of the Taylor Report and participate in curricular development in the role of informed governors. What schools do not want are parents motivated by egotistical or political stances, who consider they have a right to question and alter established school practice, with no real understanding of the philosophy behind that practice.

In this chapter, parental roles have been defined in relation to the school and its attitudes. Obviously the supportive role of the parent at home is equally applicable, and will operate to a similar degree, i.e. parents may be interested or uninterested in their children's school activities at OBSERVER level; they can help in a PRACTICAL way by providing a quiet place for homework or buying helpful books; they may take on the role of INSTRUCTOR by discussing school topics or reading with their child. Improved home/school liaison can ideally support parents, whichever role they adopt, with a parallel improvement in the child/parent/teacher relationship.

CHAPTER 3

Making parents welcome

John Rennie of the Coventry 'Community Education in Action' Project said, 'When a head tells me the door of his office is always open for parents, I know that he doesn't really want parents in the school.' Such a headteacher is only willing to meet parents on his own grounds and on his own terms. If we believe that parents are partners in the educational process, then we must take positive steps to make them welcome. Many parents have uncomfortable memories of their own schooling, with teachers whose classrooms were sacrosanct, whose word was law, and who never considered it part of their job to collaborate with parents. We hope that we are beginning to understand that the education of a child is a partnership between the teacher and the parent.

Many of us pay lipservice to the idea, but find it hard to put into practice. Are we to have parents wandering round the school at any time? Do we want to be exposed to what may be ill-informed scrutiny and criticism? Our job is difficult enough without having to cope with the many parents who do not understand what we are doing, who may think of us as left-wing agitators who have far too much holiday. Many parents question our methods, and believe that our informal child-centred ways of teaching necessarily produce lower standards than those which they achieved. 'Why don't our children learn their tables?' they cry; 'What happened to grammar? Don't you teach them to spell any longer? This practical Maths is all very well, but it just looks like playing to me.'

In our experience, parents who are welcomed into the classroom, who are shown what we do and why, become enthusiasts. They are grateful for the opportunity to understand what their children learn and how. They enjoy taking part in the process, and they see that happy confident children learn better than cowed and submissive ones. Almost without exception, the parents we know who have become involved in shared reading have become interested in and supportive of their child's school. There are many practical ways of making this happen, and as we have stressed before, each school will find its own way of involving parents and organizing the curriculum to include them. Here are some of the ways we have made parents welcome in our own schools.

Getting to know parents before their children come to school

If you have a nursery class attached to your school, you are very fortunate. It is then comparatively easy for the reception class teacher, literacy co-ordinator or headteacher to meet parents as soon as their children join the nursery. If not, look for your nearest playgroup or mothers and toddlers group. Try to get to know the playgroup leaders, perhaps even join the committee, turn up to their social and fund-raising events, then you will have already begun to meet parents in an informal setting. If possible meet the children whenever you can; try to beg time from your head to spend half an hour in the playgroup or nursery, even if it only happens once a month. Ask if you can read the children a story, learn their names, make sure that your face is familiar to them. If you do this you will find that many parents will talk to you spontaneously about ways of preparing their children for the first day in school. Parents like to know what will be expected of their child, what skills you like them to bring to school. Some schools have a letter with a list of those skills, such as the ability to dress and undress oneself, cope with the loo, recognize colours, enjoy using paint and glue, and manipulate scissors.

If you have already established a friendly relationship with parents, you may find they will ask you what they can do to help with reading, counting and writing. Many parents have said to us that they are anxious not to do the 'wrong' thing. At this point it may be helpful to organize a meeting of prospective parents with the support of the nursery teacher or playgroup leader. It is important to choose a time when parents are free. Perhaps you could have a meeting when parents come to collect children at the end of the morning, or in the evening at a book-selling party in someone's home.

This is the time to talk about the 'partnership' element in their child's education, and show them how they can help their children to enjoy books. Some of the parents may not be involved in nursery or playgroup activities, and it may be helpful to meet them at home or in some local meeting place like the pub or community centre. It is, we think, important to extend your welcome to all the parents whose children will be starting school.

Some of the questions parents ask at this stage will help you to establish positive attitudes to books long before the child begins school. If parents like to do some background reading, we have found it helpful to give them a booklist, and to keep a copy of the books we find useful on a special shelf, for loan to anyone interested.* We particularly recommend Butler's *Babies Need Books* and Bradman's *Will You Read Me a Story?*, which help parents to understand what kinds of book children will enjoy at each stage of their development, and explain how to make the bedtime story enjoyable for the whole family.

Parents who know that you are enthusiastic about their sharing of books with their children will ask you which books to buy, and where. Some parents

* Parents' booklist is at the end of Chapter 7.

may not know which books are appropriate for pre-school children, and many of them want to buy reading scheme books or phonic-based puzzle books. You have a golden opportunity to organize a bookclub or a visit from the local library. We have found local bookshops only too happy to bring along books for display at a coffee morning. It is not easy for a busy parent with toddlers to visit a bookshop, and many parents need to see what books are available in comfort, free from the anxiety of struggling with shopping and lively children in pushchairs. Bookshops are regrettably not always designed with toddlers in mind.

Parents also like to be given some help and guidance on how to help their child with writing. Most children will experiment with marks on paper long before they come to school. Parents wonder whether to use capital or lower case letters. It is very disheartening for a child who can write her name in capitals to be told that 'we don't do it like that in school'. There is some interesting research by Bissex and others to show that capital letters are much easier to form than lower case letters, and yet we have usually discouraged children from using capitals as soon as they begin school. We think that parents may well have something to contribute to the debate, and we recommend that children should be praised and encouraged for all their attempts to write, and that parents should understand that we welcome such praise and encouragement.

One parent of a pre-school child confessed to the reception class teacher that she was very worried because her child was already reading. She was afraid that the child would have to begin at the beginning of the reading scheme and would get bored. When the teacher expressed delight in the child's achievements, and explained her enthusiasm for using a wide variety of books, and for partnership with parents, the mother was very relieved, and offered to come into school to share books with other children. The teacher was fortunate in being able to work with someone who had already succeeded in helping a child to read and was willing to share her time and expertise with other children.

Explaining your methods

As soon as children are settled in the reception class we like to begin our shared reading system. There are many ways of doing this, and we describe some of them in the next chapter. We have already established warm and welcoming relationships with parents, and we feel that personal contact with each family is very important. We may then write a letter to all parents, in mother tongue if necessary, explaining how our system works, and what kind of feedback we would like from parents. We are careful to stress that we would like every child to share books with an interested adult. If a parent is not able to do this herself, she may well be able to suggest a neighbour, older brother or sister or grandparent.

Very few parents are unwilling to help if we take the trouble to engage them actively, but if a parent is too busy or harassed, we make sure that she understands that there will be someone to help, either in school or out. In our enthusiasm, we sometimes forget that parents have a choice, and if we have properly explained our system without revealing hidden assumptions about that parent, then we must accept the parent's decision without making her feel guilty. As long as the child has what Clark called 'one interested adult who has time to devote to that particular child', we know that the child will have confidence in the partnership.

After we have spoken to each parent, we may then organize a meeting at a time when parents are free. It's no good asking people to come when they are all watching *EastEnders* or going to a local keep-fit class. You will know your parents well enough by this time, to choose a time to suit them. We may show our video, have a book display, organize coffee, perhaps ask older children to read with the new parents, or even demonstrate by role play the most effective ways of sharing books with children.

We ask parents to look for the gradual development of reading strategies as their children progress. Waterland's chart of reading skills is very helpful, and we show parents how we keep records with our own reading profile, so that they understand our careful monitoring system. We also point out some of the dangers of pushing too hard, choosing inappropriate times for sharing books, or stressing too narrow a phonic approach. We found parents responded with amusement and recognition to the Gateshead video of 'Dennis' from *Auf Wiedersehen Pet* demonstrating good and bad practice. When parents feel that they are active partners, we know that this has not happened by accident. It takes time and hard work to keep up that all-important individual contact.

Written communication

If you are going to send letters and leaflets out to parents you will already have established ways of doing this appropriate to your own community. It may help to look more carefully at the sort of language you use. Is it designed to be read easily by all parents? How attractively is it presented? Are you sure that all your messages get to the right destination? We found the work of the University of Nottingham School of Education very helpful. The researchers looked at the many ways in which schools communicated with parents, and as a result, produced three useful booklets. One of them looked at the initial training of teachers and considered what help students are given on initial training courses in learning to relate to parents. Most of us will have been given very little guidance, and will have had to learn by experience.

One booklet studies interviews arranged by teachers for parents, and the way we perceive each other. The third booklet is entitled 'Written Communication between Home and School' and gives many examples of brochures and letters sent out from schools. If we are to make parents feel welcome in schools, we must try not to put them off by using too much jargon, or by producing lists of do's and dont's which make them feel humiliated and patronized. We express the attitude of our school to parents as much in what we write as in what we say.

There are some splendid examples of good communication with parents in the booklet, with charming pictures, lively text and a welcoming tone, which indicate that the schools concerned are reaching out to the community, not slamming doors in parents' faces. Do not neglect the opportunity to let the children write invitations to coffee mornings; infants in particular will be proud to take home a letter they have written themselves. It may be just as well to check

'Its about the computer workshop'

that parents have received messages, and a quick word at the school gate may prompt a parent to come to a meeting more readily than a letter with a tear-off slip at the bottom. If you are preparing a leaflet on shared reading to hand out to parents, do make sure that it strikes a positive note, and that it is easy for parents to understand the leaflet over leaf is sent out to our schools. It has been translated for the Punjabi families who speak Punjabi at home. We are able to have it

North Herts Teachers Centre

School/Home Achieves Reading Enjoyment

SHARE – a school/home reading project

All recent research indicates that children learn to read more quickly and naturally when parents are involved. Just as they learn to talk by imitation, so they learn to read, with understanding, by copying those who read to them.

For this skill to develop the child needs:–

1. The individual support of a sympathetic adult.

2. A sense of purpose and meaning.

3. Freedom from anxiety and stress.

4. A sense of enjoyment and success.

Both teachers and parents can work together to achieve these.

SHARED READING

What Can You Do to Help?

At Home.

Your child will bring home a "book bag", containing his chosen book.

It's often a good idea to read the story first, and then to share the reading together. At first your child may only know one or two words and you can supply the rest.

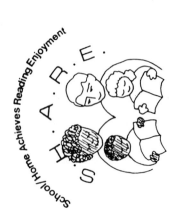

"bringing home a book bag..."

Enjoy the book together with the child sitting close to you. It helps to remember:–

– to find a quiet place, at a time when both you and your child are relaxed.

– only read for as long as the child wishes

– make sure your child can see the print and pictures, talk about the pictures they often give clues to the story.

– move your finger smoothly under the words. Talk about the story. Ask "What do you think will happen next?"

– PRAISE ALL YOUR CHILDS ATTEMPTS, whether it is reading one or two words or phrases, reading from memory or making up his own story from the illustrations.

Encourage him to practice his new skills, maybe sharing the book with other friends or members of the family. All children have favourite stories and these are often the first ones they read independently.

encourage the sharing of favourite stories

At School

Here, the teacher will be reading with your child in the same way, and ensuring that there are always plenty of good attractive story books available. She will also begin to teach the particular reading skills required as your child progresses.

Your child may also be making his own simple story books possibly using a sentence maker. When each book is complete it will be brought home to read and to keep.

Your child's teacher will be happy to show you how children learn to read and write using this method.

Later On

As your child's confidence and ability grow, you will find he is reading to you more often. At this stage the child's choice of book may vary. Occasionally he will return to familiar, simple stories because they are reassuring favourites. Another time he will choose a book which will demand more adult help.

- Continue to tell the child any new word, after giving him a few seconds to work it out. Sometimes it helps to ask what sound it begins with.

- Don't insist on absolute accuracy. Be encouraging if your child puts in a different word, and the story makes sense.

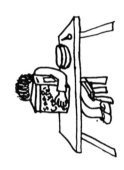

he will begin to read a variety of reading material

Encourage a variety of reading material. It may be information books on his favourite interests, cereal packets, T.V. adverts or road signs!

Once your child is reading independently, then he is well on his way to a lifetime of enjoying books. Continue to make time to share reading together. Even though your child appears to read fluently he'll still need your interest and encouragement for many years to come!

Happy Reading!

even a fluent reader still requires occasional help

translated for us by out Multi-Ethnic Support team into any of the more usual languages spoken by families in our area.

If you have organized a way for parents to respond to their children's reading progress, make sure that you read their comments and treat them with courtesy and respect. One parent who found it very difficult to talk face to face with her child's teacher entered into an informative and happy correspondence with her through the record book that went home every night.

Working with parents in school

Once you have a well-established system of taking books home for parents to share with the children, you may like to extend it. There may be parents who are willing to share books with children in the classroom, and who are happy to give other children the time and interest that they give their own children at home. It is impossible for the teacher of a large class to give each child 10 or 15 minutes with a real storybook every day. We co-opt every willing adult we can find, big sisters on the dole, neighbours, friends, pensioners, visitors, anyone who is willing to see how we work.

Some schools prefer to set aside a session once a week when parents come in, some prefer to have just one or two parents helping at a time. It is up to the individual teacher to work out what method she uses with the help of the head-teacher. There are as many ways of encouraging parents into school as there are schools. We are fortunate in having had the opportunity to see how schools in Hertfordshire have organized shared reading.

If parents come in one at a time we feel it is important not to isolate them. We like to make our morning coffee break into a social occasion, and we sacrifice the opportunity to 'let off steam' because we are glad to show our parents that we appreciate the support and commitment they give. It is true that you have to be discreet about school problems, and you may not feel so relaxed at first, but the advantages soon outweigh the disadvantages. We have made friends and won ardent supporters in this way. Parents are asked before they start working in school, to understand that we trust them not to gossip about particular children, and to respect the confidence the staff place in them. We have never yet had that confidence abused, because the parents who work with us know we respect their contribution to the school.

If you ask a group of parents to come into school to work together, you might consider making an area for them to use. We know that space is at a premium, but we take heart from Rennie again. He says that he has never yet been to a school where he could not find a corner to convert to parents' use. One school we know cornered off part of the hall and provided cushions and bookshelves. The parents brewed up in the cookery area. Another school made the staffroom available when the staff were in their classroom. One headteacher we know took a class for 15 minutes each week so that the teacher responsible for shared reading could take a coffee break with the parents and discuss the morning's reading with them.

Each school will have its own solution, and we would be glad to hear from any of you who have found novel ways of organizing classroom space and making parents feel at home. We feel that we are just beginning to realize the possibilities of taking positive action to involve parents in their children's schooling, and wonder what other areas of the curriculum might benefit from parental involvement.

CHAPTER 4

Individual practice

Preparation

The key to efficient organization of a shared reading scheme is time. Such a scheme requires hard work on the part of all the staff in a school and, because it may lead to a major change in curriculum policy, it will affect the way teachers see themselves. In this chapter we would like to look more closely at the organizational aspects of shared reading. If you are asking teachers to re-examine their methods of teaching reading, and at the same time their relationship with parents, you may need to take a long view. Teachers need to study the evidence, to discuss their doubts, to visit other schools or to take part in INSET if they are to feel comfortable and confident in what they are doing. If colleagues remain unconvinced, it may be possible to start very slowly. One school organized a pilot scheme with a group of summer-born infants who needed a little extra help with reading. This was so successful that the rest of the staff were persuaded to take part. It may be a good idea to send books home with just one class of children at first, or to ask one or two parents into school to share books with the children one day a week. While this is going on, head and staff will be able to discuss the next step without feeling rushed.

Parent governors may like to look at home/school communication, or take an interest in book provision or library furnishings. These are normal aspects of school life which may well need more attention before the adoption of a whole school policy. We feel that it is important that all the members of staff work together long before parents become involved, although this does not always happen in practice. It may take as long as five years before a flourishing shared reading policy is implemented with most parents and all teachers and children taking part. During this time, you may find that you slowly change from a school with traditional home/school co-operation to one where parental involvement is seen as 'enriching the school by enlisting the skills and knowledge of the parents, benefiting the children by improved home/school liaison, and satisfying the desire of many parents to assist in their children's education' (Tizard *et al.* 1981).

The time taken to prepare your policy is well spent if you therefore read the evidence before you begin, so that you know precisely why you are changing time-honoured methods, and are clear in your own mind of the value of what you are planning. You may need to look at the way you evaluate reading progress if you are to demonstrate that shared reading is based on sound professional principles. You may need to find out what is happening in your own area, to visit other schools, to ask for help from the advisory staff in your county, to attend or organize a course for local schools so that you have a wider forum for discussion than your own staffroom. We have been fortunate in having the opportunity to visit many schools in North Hertfordshire, and have been able to talk to parents, teachers and children who are all taking part in many ways in a shared reading programme. We have had constant help and encouragement from our Advisory Teacher for Reading, who has been able to provide us with research documents to read, and has visited many schools in our area to talk to staff and parents. We have also had the support of the Schools Library Service staff, who have coped with supplying schools with far more books than they have used before.

Reading schemes and records

Once you are sure you want to go ahead, you need to make careful plans before you launch your scheme. Are you going to continue to use your reading scheme books alongside your library books? Many parents and teachers were worried about losing the structure of the reading scheme as a measure of progress. It may be easier to run your reading scheme as a language development scheme, or keep only the books with exciting stories in and abandon the ones with contrived language and no story line. It is a good idea to use collections of reading scheme books for group reading, as schools will have several copies of the same book. Many schools begin parental involvement by sending home the reading scheme books as the schools in the Haringey project did. This has disadvantages if you want to change to a wider choice later, because parents may not want to lose sight of the progressive goals in a reading scheme. It may be helpful to show parents your record-keeping system and point out that you believe the development of good reading behaviour and the growth of fluency are better measures of progression than reliance on proceeding from Book 3 to Book 4.

Many teachers, too, have expressed the fear that they will be unable to measure progress if they let children choose books for themselves. When we talked to them at length, we found that good teachers were perfectly confident that they were able to assess the abilities of the children they taught, but they felt that they needed to respond to other people's request for some form of measurement. They felt that they needed to answer headteachers, parents, local authorities, teachers in the next class or school, inspectors and supply teachers. We suggest ways of measuring progress which we hope will satisfy all those concerned, but most of all the teacher herself.

Involving the parents

If you are ready to introduce shared reading with parental involvement into your school, you will already have spent some time discussing such a project with your colleagues, and will have decided on your own methods of assessment. You are happy with the principles of shared reading, you want parents to be partners, and you now need to look more carefully at the practical aspects of your scheme. Communicating with parents and making them welcome will be an important part of any change in school policy. If you already know the parents well, and have personal contact with them, you may find it helpful to prepare a leaflet outlining the way you would like them to share books with their children at home. This is the time to organize a workshop in school, perhaps to show parents a video and ask for their views. Some parents may wish to help in school, some may like to help their own child at home.

Parents have a right to choose what they do. If a parent prefers not to become involved it is not fair to make them feel inadequate. There should be time during the school day for their child to share books with other adults, or to see if there is someone close to the child in his own home environment who would be glad to help. All children deserve that precious time with 'one interested adult'.

Bookbags

You may need to buy bookbags and label them with the names of the children so that books can be taken to and from school safely. We use plastic bags with a zip, which we can order from County Supplies at about 20p per bag. One school made bags from scrap material, another school found their nearest YTS group making and marketing a very simple plastic bag for 9p. If you make your bookbags out of material, try machining a lining of dustbin bag material into them to make the bags waterproof. Some schools use plastic supermarket bags with the child's name written on in felt pen. We try to discourage the children from putting leaking lunchboxes in the same bag! In each bag we put the child's chosen book and a card or small exercise book so that teacher and parent can jot down comments on the popularity of the book, the fluency of the reading, and any new strategies noticed.

The teacher may tell the parent whether the book is to be read by the child, read together, or read by the parent to the child. The parent may note that the child has begun to point to each word, recognizes her own name letter, or can predict the story from the pictures. Comments do not need to be too comprehensive, but they help to develop a good working partnership. One mother was very shy and reluctant to express herself in talking to the teacher, but became much more confident in her written comments on her child's reading habits. She was able to explain how all her children had enjoyed the bedtime story, including her four-year-old who recited the Storychest book *Meanies* when he was in the bath. It is very satisfying, too, for a parent to be the first to notice a new development. The extracts below, from a record book kept in a reception class, shows how well teacher and parent are working together and understanding the child's progress.

Example pages from a record book

13 1 88 The night train. Clare might read this with you after you've read it to her. See if she can find 'Tickelty-tat' on each page.

The Night train
Clare · loves the book and would like to keep it, she gained confidence, and insisted on her doing the reading. She read it all numerous times, with little help. 'Tickelty-tats' – no problem!

Boo hoo   14/1/88

A very easy one again – faintly old-fashioned I think!
        'Boo-hoo' went down just as well as 'Tickelty-tat'. The rhymes make it easy to memorise. She had no trouble reading it alone, in fact she's so pleased with herself we often found her reading the entire book aloud on her own. Anyway, I'm getting bored with 'Boo-hoo' so can I have a new story!

18 1 88   Here another of the same sort. She'll manage it very soon, after you. Incidentally She 'read' Boo hoo beautifully to me!
        Yes, she enjoyed this one too, so much so, I caught her doing a bit of nocturnal reading at 10 o'clock last night!

20 1 88 The Party. The simplest one of all! She is doing very well.

Toad Tuesday one for you to read —
I don't know it, let me know
what you think!,

No, 'The party' wasn't all that absorbing!
As for 'Toad Tuesday', it didn't appeal
to me much - the names were a
bit hardgoing with "Ma Toad Friday and
Pa Toad Sunday' etc.. Clare didn't
show much of an interest until about
the third run through it.
They were such grumpy looking toads.

26 1 88   The red rose.   An easy
read, rather pretty, delicate
pictures.

The
red
rose

Clare liked
this one very
much and managed
to read it well
just getting
stuck on an odd
word.

We have a big cardboard box in the classroom for the children's bookbags. The children put their bags in the box at the beginning of the day, and the teacher encourages the children to choose new books and fills in the record at a suitable moment, usually when the child is free to read to her. You will need to keep a record of the books which have gone home in case any go missing. Some teachers number the books and just jot down the number in a notebook, some have a book with a page for each child. Middle and top infants and juniors are able to change their own books and note the title, and enjoy the responsibility of keeping the classroom record. They may leave the card or record book from the bag on the teacher's desk so that she can read the comments when she has time.

We like the children to change their books whenever they like, but you may prefer to set aside a couple of days a week to start with until you all get used to the system. It is no good encouraging children to change books whenever they like if you cannot keep track of what is happening, so you need to work out a system that suits you. You will probably be amazed at the number of books the children take home. One little boy with special needs took home 26 books in half a term. We asked his mother how he was enjoying them. 'Oh, I can't stop him,' she said, 'I don't think he's what you'd call reading properly, but he thinks he is.' In school the same little boy is confident enough to 'read' to any visitors from the books he knows by heart. He 'thinks he is a reader'.

A need to keep a record of books.

Book supply

You will need to look carefully at your supply of books. We find that we are spending less money on reading scheme books and more on story and information books. This obviously has implications for publishers. We look critically at what we have on our shelves and discard any books with a poor story line or contrived language. If you have too small a collection of books, you may find the children getting bored with the stock. You could exchange your books with a parallel class. We think that you need approximately three times the number of books as children in the class to begin with. We buy books from children's bookclubs, use Storychest books, and any books we already have in our classrooms. Most of all we have had great co-operation and encouragement from our Schools Library Service. It is no good beginning a shared reading scheme without making sure you have a good supply of books. It is only fair to warn your local school and county library that you will be asking for far more books than you have used in the past.

We are deeply grateful to the librarians in North Hertfordshire who have given us unstinting help, providing us with extra books and booklists, and visiting schools to share their expertise. Our librarians have been part of the team organizing shared reading workshops, they have kept us up to date with new books, replaced old and much loved copies of favourite books, and helped us to organize family reading groups. You will be using books all day and every day and in far greater numbers than ever before.

Many teachers and parents have expressed their worries that books are going to get lost or damaged. It is true that you will occasionally have to replace a book, because the most popular books simply fall apart. But an immaculate book sitting unread on a shelf is no good to anyone. Our librarians understand this and have willingly replaced worn-out favourites. We also found that the children were surprisingly careful. It seems that the interest generated by the scheme, and the fact that they made the choice of what they read, led them to value and respect their books. We only lost two in five years; one was sicked on by a dog, and the other was given to a jumble sale because it was 'so tatty'. Of course it was the classroom favourite, long past its best, and the embarrassed parent rushed out and bought us another copy straight away.

You could consider asking parents to contribute a small sum each term towards the purchase of new stock, or you could suggest that they replace lost or damaged books. You could organize a sponsored read to raise money for books as a way of launching your scheme. You could have a display of books from the Schools Library Service or local bookshop, with parents buying books for the library with a bookplate inside designed by the children. You will know best whether your parents can afford to contribute or not. It is a question of judgement, which is much easier when you know your parents better.

Classification

Do you need to classify your books into ability bands? If you feel happier with some sort of classification, you could use Moon's *Individualised Reading* scheme. Those of us who carefully sorted our books into baskets or colour coded them found that we soon began to ignore our coding. As Liz Waterland said to us, 'If a child wants to read a book from the red basket, and his reading isn't advanced enough, I simply read it to him. I don't want to say to a child, "No you can't enjoy that book yet".' Liz coded her books at first, but soon realized that she was giving herself unnecessary work. Those teachers who are a little unsure may well feel more comfortable with a coding system, and many of us began in that way, until we became confident of the children's good sense in choosing what they wanted to read and could cope with. Now we simply make a note on the record book as to the level of help the parent will provide. The child then has access to any book in the library.

'All right Prudence, if you're sure'

Children like challenges, and will often attempt a book far beyond their reading ability if they are interested enough in the content. If children are tired or not very well, they are happy to go back to old favourites, which is exactly what adults do. The only classification we make is to sort the books into groups roughly suitable for each class, although we make sure that there are plenty of picture books in the junior classrooms, and some of the 'Banana' or 'Cartwheel' series of books on the infants' shelves for those children who are beginning to read well and can manage a whole chapter.

Reading in school

We like to give ourselves and the children a period of USSR (Uninterrupted Sustained Silent Reading), every day, with teachers and welfare helpers joining in. Even the reception class children enjoy looking at picture books quietly while the teacher reads her detective story. A junior child told us he liked short stories to read in school, because the time was too short for him to get involved in the exciting novel he was reading at home. He would happily have read for an hour at a time. We stress to parents too that we cannot expect children to see the importance of reading unless we do it ourselves. One school plans a period of 20 minutes after break each morning for silent reading, and it is a strange experience to visit the school and find 80 children and all the staff reading quietly together.

We have talked elsewhere about providing an area for parents who help in school. What about the children? In a recent survey (DES/Assessment of Performance Unit Report) many children stated their preference for reading at home, where there was peace and quiet in their bedrooms, and where they could read what they wanted. One child told us she liked reading 'Not when somebody tells you, but when you are sure that nobody will ask you to read out loud, or write about what you have read.'

Is your reading area sufficiently enticing? We cannot provide perfect conditions for reading in school, but we can try to create a reading area in the hall, library or classroom, with carpets and cushions or even an old sofa like the one in Liz Waterland's classroom. One school we visited had just bought huge soft cushions with money supplied by the PTA. The children immediately lay on them and read quietly.

A successful launch

How are you going to launch your scheme? You have organized bookbags, a good supply of books, and a comfortable area in your classroom. How do you communicate with parents? We have stressed that there is no substitute for personal contact. In *School, Sweet School*, Tizard *et al.* (1981) found individual contact to be by far the most efficient and effective method of communication, and yet we often organize meetings first and find ourselves disappointed when we attract only parents who are active in the PTA, much as we appreciate their support. Some parents are daunted by rows of chairs and visiting speakers, and are unwilling to ask questions. We found that a workshop was more effective, and parents were much more willing to express themselves in small groups. Please give parents time to study the evidence, if they wish, and discuss your proposals. They may well have doubts, and will be very grateful if you show that you believe that they have a right to express those doubts to you.

If you decide to hold a meeting in school, with a video, perhaps, a book display, refreshments, or a visiting speaker, do not forget parents who are too busy or not willing to attend such a function. As we have stressed before, we think all parents should have the chance to be involved in shared reading, and there are very few who won't want to take part at one level or another. They may find evening meetings difficult to attend because they are on shift work, or cannot get a babysitter. Some mothers may prefer to come to school during the day, when younger children are in the playgroup. Know your parents, and you will know what suits them best.

Each school is unique. We are grateful to all the schools in North Hertfordshire, who invited us to share their ideas, filled in our questionnaire (below) and welcomed us into their busy classrooms. Shared reading with parental involvement takes careful planning and good communication. If you give yourselves enough time to talk and make sensible plans, teachers, parents and children will all benefit from a common aim and a closer working relationship.

Shared reading questionnaire for schools in North Hertfordshire

We are interested in finding out how useful our Share Workshops have been to teachers. If you have begun shared reading in your school we would be very grateful if you could fill in this questionnaire to help us.

Please tick the appropriate answer or answers, or put a number in the box provided.

Number of staff in school ☐

What age groups of
children are involved in
shared reading?
☐ Junior
☐ Infant
☐ Nursery

How many of your staff are
involved?
☐ Teachers
☐ Welfare helpers
☐ Nursery nurses

How many parents are
involved? ☐

How do you choose the
parents?
☐ Staff choice
☐ Parent volunteers
☐ Whole class

Where do the parents share books with the child?	☐ At home
	☐ In the classroom
	☐ In separate area

How did you introduce the idea to the parents?	☐ Teacher's individual approach to parent
	☐ Teacher organization of whole class parents' meeting
	☐ PTA/Whole school approach

What form did your introduction take? (If you did more than one, please put them in order).	☐ Letter/leaflet
	☐ Small group workshop
	☐ Outside speaker/video

How do you keep records?

Is there any opportunity for parents to comment on or discuss shared reading?

Have you any way of assessing the effect of shared reading on reading standards?

Have you any further comments you would like to make?

Would you like a copy of our findings by the end of the Spring Term?   Yes   No

If you don't mind your school being identified, please fill in this section:

    Name of School:
    Address:

Thank you for telling us what you think.

Chris Davis,
Rosemary Stubbs.

Please return this form to Chris and Rosemary at Hertfordshire College of Higher Education, Wall Hall, Aldenham, Watford WD2 8AT.

Results of questionnaire

We sent out this questionnaire to the schools in North Hertfordshire who sent members of staff to our first two SHARE workshops. Because there was a large response to the request for names of people wishing to attend the workshops, we organized a third meeting for schools in the Royston area. We were unable to include them in the statistics at the time of writing this document.

26 schools sent members of staff to the first two workshops.
62 teachers attended
1 school was unable to attend but started shared reading with our help, and sent in a return.

Of the 27 schools we canvassed:
20 sent in replies to our questionnaire.
2 schools are still intending to fill it in, and 5 schools have not replied.

Number of schools who have already begun shared reading schemes	14
Number of schools who have made plans to begin shortly	3
Number of schools who do not intend to begin shared reading	2
Number of schools who did not wish to fill in the questionnaire	1

These are the results we obtained including those from schools who had already made detailed plans and had discussions with those involved.

Number of staff involved in shared reading	Teachers	63
	Welfare helpers	12
	Nursery nurses	9
Number of parents involved in shared reading	In school	Approx. 100
	At home (approx.)	600 +

Number of schools involving Junior classes	7
Number of schools involving Infant classes	15
Number of schools involving Nursery classes	7
Number of schools where staff choose parents	4
Number of schools where parents volunteer	7
Number of schools where whole classes are involved	5
Number of schools where parents read at home	15
Number of schools with parents in classroom	10
Number of schools with parents in separate area	6

Number of schools using individual approach   6
Number of schools using whole class approach   6
Number of schools using whole school approach   11

Number of schools sending out letter/leaflet   13
Number of schools organizing small group workshop   6
Number of schools arranging outside speaker/video   12

It should be noted that many schools used more than one approach.

All the schools organizing shared reading kept records of the books going home.

All the schools organizing shared reading had some way of getting feedback from parents, 5 schools used cards or exercise books for written feedback, 9 schools has personal contact with parents.

Methods of assessment

No formal method: 9
Liz Waterland chart: 2
Control group: 2
Monitoring using Young's test and Neale's Analysis: 1

All the schools who were already using a shared reading system were sure that the children were more enthusiastic about books, and were making more progress with their reading, but were anxious to organize some form of continuous assessment alongside a standardized reading test. We replied to this request by producing our reading profile which we reproduce in Chapter 6.

CHAPTER 5

Individual perceptions

We asked parents taking part in shared reading in two schools with well-established schemes to fill in a questionnaire so that we could see how successful shared reading had been from the parents' point of view. Of the 14 parents who filled in the questionnaire, we found none who were unwilling to complete it. These are the results:

	more	about the same	less
Do you feel your child enjoys books?	9	5	0
Do you feel that your child is reading?	9	5	0
Do you feel that your child is understanding books?	10	4	0

	Yes	No
Do you feel that you have more idea of the sort of books your child enjoys?	13	1

	more	about the same	less
Do you feel that you understand how children learn to read?	8	6	0
Do you feel able to help your child?	8	6	0

How often do you share books with your child?		
every evening		3
most days		6
2 or 3 days a week		5

Where do you get books from?		
library		9
bookshop		7
other shop		6
school		14

We talked to many parents who came to workshops organized in school, and we asked for further comments on the questionnaire. We were very impressed with the response of parents, who were grateful for the opportunity to tell us what they felt. We felt sad that teachers often ignore this wealth of well-informed or questioning response.

On the choice of books

We'd like teachers to have more say in the choice of books children bring home. We feel we need more guidance. Perhaps you could have a colour coding or grading, and the children could choose from their colour.

I feel the scheme is very beneficial, but would like the book choice supervised more closely. Many of the books are chosen time and time again and the children do tend to become bored with some of the books.

On the reading process

I find she selects words and then hangs other words around it.

She knows the story, but doesn't take the word out of context in another situation.

We still think phonetics has a place. What about the rules of reading?

Should they go on reading aloud? Yes, because it teaches them to read with expression.

When they read at home and don't know a word, do you sound it out or just say it?

The teacher explained that the parent should supply the word so that the sense of the text was not lost. The parents burst into relieved laughter, and had a discussion about the difficulty of sounding out words in English.

My older child learnt with flashcards and reading scheme books. He doesn't read as well as my other younger children who do it by sharing. He finds reading boring.

On the enjoyment of reading

Sharing reading with us Mums makes school more exciting.

Are there any books you wouldn't recommend, like comics or Enid Blyton?

The teacher pointed out that most avid readers of her generation read Enid Blyton and enjoyed comics. She suggested that as long as the child enjoyed the book and was not too frightened or disgusted by it, she would not censor what he read.

I think it's important to enjoy the book without being too analytical about the vocabulary.

My child has always enjoyed books, and because she has more of her own choice, she mostly likes to read the books herself now.

Karen has always been a good reader, and I'm sure that the 'share' system has helped her, and I feel that if a child is brought up to appreciate books from an early age there are fewer problems.

When I ticked 'about the same' on the questionnaire it was because my child has always had an interest in reading different types of book from quite an early age, and we have tried as parents to respond whenever possible.

This project seems to be extremely worthwhile. Saradia enjoys being able to choose books frequently, but in her own time, allowing her to enjoy reading. She is sharing not only with family at home, but is given an opportunity for discussion at school with friends.

We have always shared books together as a family, but I think Nick enjoys being able to choose for himself whatever book he likes as often as he likes.

On home arrangements

I do feel it is a good idea to enjoy books with your child. But a working Mum like me doesn't have enough time to share books.

It's hard to find time for each of them when you have three children.

It's important to start them off at home early, before they come to school.

I would rather be guided by the teacher as to how I can help them at home. The worry is, am I doing the right thing? Is it OK that I read a lot to her, should I make her read more?

I find it hard to find time. Is it alright for her to read on her own?

The teacher suggested they could talk about the books she reads. Perhaps there is a Granny or Aunty who isn't out at work who would like to share reading.

Well I think the situation at home needs guidance, the atmosphere is wrong, with telly and younger children. When we saw the video, we thought perhaps the background noise didn't matter as much as teachers say, because that classroom was quite noisy.

Is five minutes a day enough?

I think it's important to have a quiet time with your child.

It's excellent, it gives me a sit-down.

On parental help with reading in school

I think this one hour as a group parent session is a good idea, providing it went from the beginning of school.

I'd prefer to help in another class, not in my child's class.

We think the hour in school is a great idea.

Parental involvement in school is important, but we must all be working towards the same goal.

There needs to be more parental involvement.

You see the other side of your children. What we see at home is not what we see in school.

I think it's better in school because of the competition.

If we could start it as a pilot idea in the juniors, there would be more wanting to take part as it took off.

It can only work when teachers and parents liaise properly.

On the wider implications of parental involvement in the curriculum

It gives us an open door into what happens in school. If there were any problems we'd know sooner.

I think it's a good idea so long as teachers don't put their responsibility on to parents.

Yes, parents should have a say in the curriculum.

How useful are parents' comments? How much notice do teachers take of what we say?

We're concerned for new Mums. They don't understand the overall aims of the system. They need to have the structure broken down and explained to them. No information has filtered through.

This was because the teacher who normally introduced shared reading was on secondment to do this work. It showed the importance of making sure supply teachers understand the system!

We ought to get together to discuss things like – well – I heard children shouldn't learn to read until they're six. What do you think?

It would be a good idea if parents could spend a morning in the first class when their child first goes to school, then they could have the reading methods explained to them.

Perhaps parents of playgroup children could be helped with ideas for helping children before they come to school, like – should we teach them the alphabet?

It's a good idea to find out individual parents' abilities and utilize them to the full.

It's important to help through the full curriculum, not just craft work.

There's a certain barrier with some parents who are unwilling to offer to help. They might help if they were asked, but they may be frightened of being asked to do more than they are capable of.

There is some feeling that there is a clique of 'newcomers' to the village who are the chosen few. It's not widespread, but some people feel this.

At this point we'd like to introduce a transcript of a much longer talk with two mothers from one of the village schools. They both volunteered to talk, and were interviewed by a teacher they had not met.

Transcript: discussion on parental involvement

R. Thank you for volunteering, Brenda and Janet. I'd like to hear how you feel about being involved either in school or at home. How long have you been helping in the classroom, Janet?

J. I've helped here for about three years but I've helped in different schools for about nine or ten years now. In differing capacities from listening to reading, a similar sort of thing to helping the less able with work cards – that side of it – to doing some practical maths, doing volume, things which are larger and smaller – that sort of thing.

R. I know, that's really super.

J. It's great fun. Yes and in doing sewing here it's enabled me to learn an enormous amount.

R. That's nice to think that you've got something from it too.

J. I just have to stay one step ahead of them in this game!

R. Is there anything you've been asked to do that you feel you would prefer not to do?

J. No. I've enjoyed all of it. I mean even sometimes after break, sometimes I'll help with the younger ones but other times, if a wall needs stripping off, I'll do that, I mean I'm prepared to help in any way because I know how hard-pressed teachers are and how time is really at a premium: so I'm prepared to do anything that helps out in any way.

R. Good. How long have you been helping Brenda?

B. Ever since Richard started school. Two terms. I've been doing cooking and then I took over on the reading side, and I do play maths games with them… Yes and I'm helping Mrs Trollope at the moment – she needs a lot of help.

R. Oh yes, she's got a lot of new little ones, hasn't she?

B. I feel it is important for all parents to help their children. I've learnt a lot. I'm looking at books a lot better now than I ever did before. I spend a lot more time choosing the right ones.

R. That's nice. I think we're the same. It's really only over the last few years that we've stopped using just reading books for teaching reading and once you start using all those lovely story books, it makes you very fussy about books doesn't it? Have you got any younger children at home?

B. Yes I've got a daughter as well, who is at nursery school, and she's as forward as Richard because, you know, she's there when Richard has his time – I can't separate them. They join in together and I find that they compete against each other to be first so they share.

R. That's lovely. So you really think that's helped her?

B. Yes.

R. Do you think that means that you're doing things with her that you perhaps wouldn't have thought of doing with Richard before he came to school?

B. Yes. I now spend a lot more time with them. It's good because it gives a mum a chance for a sit-down! To sit and relax and have ten minutes with the children, instead of saying, 'Go away, I haven't time to read that.' I'm more likely to say come on, let's read it together.

R.   Do you feel, now that both of you have been involved very practically, and also in a teaching way… how would you feel if you were called in and asked what you thought about different aspects of the curriculum? For instance, how you considered we should teach maths? Or the way we should look at reading? Do you feel that you are in a better position to be involved on that sort of side? You know that the government are introducing more parent governors. This is the trend, isn't it? Do you think this is the best way of parents becoming governors?

J.   I think it is very important for parents to air their views about it. In an ideal world everybody would have a headmaster and a staff like we've got here, who are absolutely super and parents could give their views and I personally would trust them – I think most of the parents would trust them implicitly that they would gather together the views and would make a good valued assessment, listening to everybody's opinions because I do think that they are in a far better position than most parents to assess. But that doesn't mean that I wouldn't want to have my say. I would very much like to do that, but of course not all schools are like that, and that's where the problems occur, I think. I know from having one in a different school that a lot of schools pay lip-service to using parental help. But not all of them think it is such a wonderful idea and that even within schools there are those who think it's a good idea and those who don't. And I'm sure they think that parents don't notice, but they do! You know exactly when you're really wanted there and you know exactly when you're there just so they can say they have so many parents who come in and help. And I think that's a very important thing that you actually feel you're making – it doesn't matter whether it's a big or small contribution – that you're making a real contribution, and that you're actually wanted there; that the staff want you there as much as you want to be there. I think that's one of the most vital things.

R.   Yes. I know that you've been coming into schools for a long time. These attitudes of parents and staff have probably built up over a long period of time.

J.   I'm sure you're right.

R.   You know, I'm sure it's quite different for some teachers to accept parents in, if they are not used to it.

J.   I'm sure it must be. If they are used to being on their own with the children, then all of a sudden you're being watched. It must be quite difficult.

R.   Yes, being on the other side of the fence I don't mind because as I said, with a large class I just know that I can do my job that much better, with an extra pair of hands, using others with time to talk to the children about things like practical maths, for example.

J.   As long as it stays like that, and the teacher has everything under her responsibility all the time.

R. Absolutely.

J. I mean when we bring them in at nine o' clock, they are the teacher's responsibility – we just come in and help and we're second to the teacher. The teacher's the most important person in the classroom. The parents have to defer to the teacher.

R. Yes, I see my role as classroom manager, doing all the planning and organization.

J. Yes, I'm sure that comes across anyway to the children. If for instance, a child comes up and asks if they can go and do something, then it's a matter of pure authority whether or not you can tell them to do it. Even though I may know that Chris'll say 'Yes, they can go to the toilet', I'll always say, 'go and ask Mrs Davis'. You know I don't feel it's my place to be able to tell them whether they can do this or not.

B. Well, I've taken it upon myself to help with two children who are having problems.

J. It's a bit different with the younger ones I think.

B. She's asked me to watch them, you know, and she's delegated it to me to do that.

R. I'm finding that it's taking a lot of encouragement to get some of our parents, not only to come in but to see how valuable it is to support their children at home. I don't know whether you have any ideas how we can involve these parents more?

J. We were talking about this in our group just now, and a statement that was made which I must admit had never occurred to me before was that – this was one of the mums that walks up – she comes in to help as well (she walks up), and she says there is a certain feeling – it's not widespread – that there is like a clique in the village of people who come into school.

B. I know, I've jumped out of the clique.

R. That's a shame.

J. I know, I've never even thought about it before.

B. Yes. It all depends what part of the village you live in. The Health Visitor pointed that out to me.

R. Really.

J. That's awful. It just never occurred to me.

R. Yes. I mean the invitation is there for everyone. We don't say, 'Would you like to come in?' It's definitely anybody.

J. That's right. Well I wasn't really asked. Me being pushy, when we came here, having been in school for so many years, I just said 'if you need a helping hand, I'll come in'. I think the only way to overcome it is by individual invitation, perhaps at parents' evenings; I mean we don't get a great deal come to AGM so you can't do it like that. It has to be on a one-to-one. The other point which was made which I think is valid is that some parents are a little bit frightened that they are going to be asked to do more than they are capable of. For instance if they are dreadful at maths they are going to be asked to do something to do with maths. They want to be asked to do specific tasks or to be asked what they would prefer to do – a more individual approach.

R. Having had parents in helping with maths, I don't think they realize that a lot of it is actually just talking about what you do, isn't it? That's all the children need to help them really understand what they are doing.

B. Yes, whenever I come in to help with maths it's just playing games.

J. Um, it wasn't recognized when we were kids that maths could be like that. To me it was so dreadfully boring and it's only since coming back and helping that I've realized that it's really quite fun!

B. I'll tell you what happened with me. I met another mum when Richard first started school, and she was coming in and she said to me, 'I've been playing with Richard'. So I said, 'Oh what have you been doing?' because I didn't really know what went on in the classroom, you know, what's happening to my little boy inside the classroom. She said, 'I've been playing Snakes and Ladders'. And with that I went home, got a Snakes and Ladders and we played. All of a sudden I was introduced to what was happening in school and I was being part of his school life. I didn't like the idea of being pushed out at 9 o'clock in the morning and him not coming home until 3 o'clock.

J. That's the thing actually, although it doesn't apply in this instance, but it's something with my elder son having gone on to senior school – you feel so cut off from their school life that it's really hard. You know, having been involved since my elder son started school. It's terribly hard to come to terms with that, that all you really get is the once-a-year parents' evening and your report at the end of term. I mean I look at books in between time, we discuss it a lot. But nevertheless it's not the same involvement and can't be. It's the way they're structured.

R. It's a distance thing and it's also a maturity thing too, isn't it? I mean, they don't actually want you to be involved quite so much.

J. I haven't found that actually, though I'm sure that does occur. My son, who's almost fourteen, still likes to come home and chat things over.

B. My son is totally the opposite. He can never remember anything that's happened at school. So now I have the ability to be inside the room, to see the workings of it and then I've got that contact with Richard, as he's growing up.

J. And probably because you can discuss with Richard knowing what's going on, you'll probably find this increases as he gets older.

B. I've noticed that within the last term he has opened out an awful lot since reading and I'm able to talk with him in a way I never dreamed I'd be able to, because he's got more confidence. And having been there it gives the parents more confidence.

R. And we all know, don't we that once they're reading confidently the world is their oyster, isn't it?

J. I found it super fun having babies and teaching them things – you know everyday stuff.

B.   But the actual seeing of your work come together, I mean I bought Richard a book about going to the zoo. And he kept asking 'Can we read it? Can we read it?' Then he went off and came back and said 'Come on, mum, I'm going to read you a story'. You know, the actual thing had come together. It made it all worthwhile. Parents have to see it to believe it. I mean a lot of parents think that school is the place for schoolwork, but to actually be in school and see all your efforts come together – I mean I'm there watching 16 children learn to read now.

R.   I think it's lovely that you see it like that because to us, now that we involve parents more, it just seems so natural; in fact I was reading a list the other day of all the things parents teach children during the first five years of their life – feeding, walking, talking, etc. The amount of learning that's taken place is tremendous, so that it seems criminal in a way, that at five years old we should say, 'Right, you've done your bit. The school will take over now'. It just seems so natural to either involve the parents or for us to carry on in a similar sort of way, as much as we can.

B.   Yes, you never see it in any other age group. The younger group are so enthusiastic, as if they want to take it all in. You never capture it again. As soon as they start school, there's so much to draw in. To see it actually happening is marvellous.

R.   Yes, there are very few children that you can't interest one way or another, are there?

J.   That's right. If it's interesting enough and they're enjoying it. I think it's wonderful now that there isn't this division between home and school, that school is just as much fun as being at home. Years ago that wasn't the case and it isn't the case now with secondary schools – there's still a big division there but I think that in junior schools it is so much more relaxed. Everything is presented in a way that is actually applicable to the children. Whereas I remember learning things as a child and thinking, 'What on earth has this got to do with me?'

R.   Yes. Fortunately secondary schools are changing, and I think you'll find with the new GCSE work will become more practical, with more continuous assessment.

J.   Yes, I still feel that there is still a division, however good or bright the child is, it's nevertheless a big division.

B.   You don't get them waking up on a Saturday morning, saying, 'Aren't we going to school today?' It's harder in a secondary school because you can't have the same child/teacher contact when there are so many teachers involved. They can't always get instant praise like 'Good boy', because work has to be taken in to be marked.

R.   Exactly. But we're hoping that having been closely involved in the primary school, parents will continue to show the same interest and support through the secondary school stage.

J.   I'm sure that they will. And I've found that I now have more confidence in discussing things with my son's secondary school teachers. I'm a lot more confident at actually talking to teachers now. I think that's one of the biggest things that it's given me.

B.   And me.

R.   Good. So you really think we're beginning to break down the barriers which have existed, there's no doubt about that.

B.   I'll tell you what we didn't see on the video. The idea of putting the child on your lap and enjoying the story together, without shouting and telling them off when they're fidgeting. Now we've got a different approach – the proper approach and learning has become so much easier. And it's so much more enjoyable for us and I think the new mums don't realize this yet.

R.   Yes, I agree, perhaps we should have shown a bit more of the beginning of the tape, showing how that dad spends plenty of time with his son on his lap, really sharing the story and talking about the pictures.

B.   Last term we saw the other tape which showed us the right way to do it. This is the chance to have that contact with their children, right from the beginning. You've got to have a force between you, to have them on your lap.

J.   I quite agree, it's a very intimate thing. Being together and enjoying each other's company with a book. I still read to my children and they love it. He's 5′9″, but they enjoy it still. And I do. I love being read to, whether it's a story on the radio or if they're reading to me, whatever. And I'm now finding that in reading some of the books that I know and love we can discuss these together. And part of his course at the moment is actually the writing of a novel. And he'll write a chapter and come down and show it to me and say, 'What do you think?' or 'What about the use of this word?' It's a great sharing which is a development of the shared reading.

R.   That's great isn't it? It's so much a part of it, being exposed to so much more print they really come to understand how people write books, perhaps how you may get a descriptive part which is leading you up to an exciting part. The ups and downs that keep your attention. There's nothing to beat a book that you just can't put down, is there? I'm sure Chris would be fascinated to see the end product.

Talking to teachers

We also talked to many teachers. Some of them had only just started shared reading, some had been involving parents in school for several years.

> The enthusiasm is self-evident from the children's response. We are committed to making it work, and feel sure it will filter through from the Infant classes.

> We feel heartened by our launch of shared reading in the nursery and infants classes.

> We have no formal method of assessment yet but indications are that the children are more interested in books, and also that their fluency has improved.

We think involving parents in their children's reading is crucial. The older children really enjoy sharing books with the younger children.

We need to structure records and have some means of assessing shared reading.

We have no set test, only a feeling that children who do participate in S.H.A.R.E. are progressing quickly and reading sooner.

We taped a discussion with a group of teachers who had been using shared reading methods for over a year. These teachers all worked at the same village school, where parental involvement and the use of 'real' books was already established before their arrival. It is interesting to observe how these individual teachers adapted to this approach, having come from diverse teaching backgrounds.

Discussion between interviewer C. and Deputy Head S.

C. Now can you tell me, when you first came here, what happened?

S. In Carmarthen, I'd been used to the Ladybird reading scheme, so really, a very rigid structure, it was just the reading scheme we were using. I think the head in that school thought that it had done its job well over the years and, really, why change it, and quite honestly I was getting rather... it really was just too limiting. Storybooks in the classroom were just that, to be heard, not to be read, you know. I was quite disgusted really at it, there would have been need of doing something radical soon.

C. And no other reading scheme in that school?

S. They did have Wide Range later on in the school, top infant level, going on into the juniors.

C. Did they have a library system, or any system of borrowing books?

S. Yes, we had a library of sorts, a library in each classroom basically, and mine could take books home if they would like to. There was no system.

C. Any system of parents coming in? Helping at home?

S. None at all actually.

C. And how did you feel when you came here?

S. It was quite a shock to the system actually, to start with, realizing, you know, that you could be involved in every aspect, and having to take an initiative in the classroom was frightening, but very very rewarding as we went on, and you gained more confidence. You could branch out into so many avenues that you thought you'd not be allowed to.

C. So the first thing you noticed was that you had freedom as a teacher, to develop the curriculum in ways that you felt were appropriate?

S. That's right, yes, really, the enthusiasm had been stifled up to then, you were able to give vent to it.

C. Oh that's lovely! And did you notice what was going on with the reading? Was it obvious?

S. Oh we had talked about it in staff meetings before I'd started, and really, in the first few weeks I was just feeling my way and I felt happier just to keep to the basic reading schemes to start with, and then as I felt more confident we could branch out into other reading methods. We had One Two Three and Away, and Ginn 360 that were here before, and I used them to start with, then with Storychest we could involve other classes.

C. Who ordered Storychest then?

S. Well I think Carola and Helen in the last few years had looked very thoroughly at it and had just launched it in school, and then felt it was up to every teacher to do as they wanted with the scheme and use it in their way.

C. Did you notice any difference in the children's reading behaviour?

S. Yes. I think the most obvious change was that they were readers from the start. They didn't feel that they were... that they had to learn to read, they could just get a book and enjoy it. And just the confidence and enthusiasm that came from it at the beginning was just so uplifting, really.

C. And you start straight away as soon as they come into school?

S. Yes, and I like to read some of the stories first, especially some of the Storychest ones to start with, lovely little stories in their own right, but yet at the children's level, real life situations and imaginative situations, the sort of things that appeal to children. I think you give them an insight into the world they can get into, and what they can enjoy, whet the appetite.

C. I wanted to ask, I don't want to make it sound as though it's all wonderful, have you found anything difficult about it?

S. I think initially, really, just seeing what stage children were at, keeping a bit of a track, but I think as you became more au fait with it, you yourself can just gauge how to go about it. That was my first difficulty, really.

C. The difficulty is taking away the structure, isn't it, of a standardized reading scheme.

S. That's right, yes.

C. If you haven't got a very obvious structure, I think a lot of teachers find that daunting at first. It's a good idea to go slowly, but if you come new to a school that's already working in this way, then you haven't any option.

S. That's where it helped me, using the basic reading scheme to start with but yet using everything that was in the classroom, and now we've turned all about and are using the reading scheme books in the Storychest mode. It all works perfectly well.

C. Do you do any classifying at all?

S. Not really, no. I do find sometimes that children wish to take the same sort of book, you know, stories that they've enjoyed, and they want to take those home all the time, I do try to keep an eye on that aspect, and try to suggest something, 'Oh, this is a good book, I wonder if you'd like to enjoy this?'

C. Give a bit of a push.

S. Yes, give a bit of a push sometimes, as it's needed, but no, I don't classify.

C. Have you noticed any other spinoffs, in the writing for instance?

S. I think it leads to imaginative work. I find that children, because they have the repetition in the stories, but it isn't stilted, you use new vocabulary all the time. I think it's these sorts of spinoffs. They use some proper vocabulary, even at this early stage.

C. Because it's rhythmical, it's easy for them to understand those words, they fit in quite naturally, there isn't the old stilted vocabulary.

S. It all makes it seem very natural.

C. There's no doubt about it, when you talk to the children, they're very confident about their reading. They enjoy talking about it.

S. Oh they do, they love to go and read to others. 'Look at me, I'm reading, I'm a good reader.'

C. How about the parental involvement aspects of it? Have you done much about that yet?

S. Yes, we have two parents that come in and hear readers, and I find it works very well actually. I like to hear the children in a long session each week. It's quite a job to get them all in.

C. How many have you got in your class?

S. Twenty-three, now, I can just about manage. But I try to find the time. I have a Mum come in on a Wednesday afternoon and one on a Thursday afternoon, and they do all the spare reading. As long as I hear the children at least once, in a long 15-minute session, any extra is a bonus, because that's what they need, the practice, the enjoying of stories, and I think Mums can do that so well.

C. What about the welfare helper?

S. Yes, she comes in. We don't have any fixed time at the moment. As jobs allow she comes in, and we all share out.

C. How did you find parents? How did you decide which parents, did you decide or did they offer?

S. They offered actually, they tend to be people who come in and ask, 'Oh is there anything I could do to help?' That was really in the early stages, where I felt that the children needed to settle perhaps first, so I said, 'Yes, that would be super, perhaps we'll do it in a few weeks' time', then I've remembered them a few weeks later, and we've had a little discussion and gone ahead. There's one Mum now who's helping with some art work, and that remains to be seen because the child started crying yesterday. That hasn't happened when they've come in to help with reading.

C. I think I usually give it about a week and see if the child eventually settles, or ask the parent if they'd like to work with another class.

S. That's right, yes. But it's super, because we're all here for the same purpose, to help children, I think it's lovely that we can all mix together, and help in the same way.

C. Did you do anything to show the parents how you wanted things done, make any rules and regulations about coming into school?

S. Really, no, they just sat with us, for example, in Silent Reading period, and just saw how we did it, how the children would read, to each other, or read with me, or look at pictures and discuss what was happening in a particular picture, and from that, just explaining exactly what Storychest was all about, the philosophy behind it.

C. And they understood that?

S. They have, yes.

C. And there's no sounding out, prompting the children, 'You knew that word yesterday?'

S. There doesn't seem to be at all. They seem to be very patient and, you know, loving people who will help the children.

C. And that wonderful space, the time they can give a child.

S. Yes, the one-to-one, especially with some children who need a little bit of backup.

C. What about confidentiality, do you feel alright about that, talking about the children outside, anything like that?

S. I've had no problems. I haven't brought it up, maybe I've been just lucky, the parents who have offered to help and are willing to help in any way, they all seem to be the same ones, really very supportive, who know exactly what's going on, I'm happy about it, I like to feel that they can come to me, rather than go outside.

C. So that over the months you've developed a reasonable relationship with them, you feel you could talk to them?

S. That's right, I feel they can come to see me, first thing in the morning or whenever... they can always come in and have a chat, I feel that with the reception class, that's so important, and that is the time when you can actually get that relationship off the ground.

Discussion between interviewer C. and H.

C. Could you explain to me about the way you teach reading? First of all, tell me about the age group of the children you teach.

H. Right. I've got middle and top infants. We've got the Storychest books from Stage 2 upwards to, well some of the Stage 9 books. We choose books from the library, which is all round the classroom, and I've got 2 boxes of books with the Storychest books in, Tiddlywinks and so on, because when I have Mums in I find it's easier just to give them a box, and the children would choose from there.

C. And they'd take the children outside would they?

H. Yes, it's more peaceful. It's normally in the afternoon that I find most time to hear the children, and it's much more peaceful outside the classroom.

C. And how many mothers have you got helping you?

H. Three regularly, two come on a Monday afternoon and one on a Thursday morning.

C. How did you decide on those mothers?

H. We just ask mothers at the beginning of term. I've got one Mum who comes in and does cooking because she doesn't feel able to do reading. She's an extra pair of hands.

C. Did you do anything in the way of training them or showing them how to do it?

H. Two of them are teachers.

C. [Laughs] Well... they might be a bit inclined to do it... you know...

H. Yes, but in fact they're very keen on shared reading, they feel it's done their children a lot of good, and they share that with the other mothers.

C. Do the children take bookbags home?

H. Yes, we take our books, we haven't actually, we don't run to bags.

C. I suppose you'll have to save some money for that. And do the books survive? Do they get lost at all?

H. Oh no, not at all, and we try to do it every day. Not all the children change their books every day, I tend to mark it in my mark book when they bring one back. They take one home then that evening. Sometimes they say 'I've finished a book but I've forgotten it, so they bring back two next time.'

C. Yes, so long as you know the child is going to bring it back eventually. And what's your recording system in the classroom?

H. I've got two systems, with the reading records, when I hear them read I put that in my mark book, a red tick when I've heard them, and a black tick when a parent or other person's heard them. Then I mark down in an exercise book which books they take home.

C. Do you have any sort of system yet for feedback from parents who are hearing children read at home?

H. Not a proper one. The parents are free to come around, they come in in the morning and often say, 'Oh we enjoyed that one.'

C. So you do get some idea of how the book's gone down?

H. Yes, a verbal one.

C. And you're not asking parents to look for specific reading strategies, or anything like that?

H. No.

C. How long have you been doing it now?

H. A year last September, and we've been doing it ever since I came.

C. Did you know about it beforehand?

H. I was in a middle school, and we used to have it on a different level, but yes, we used to have the children taking books, and silent reading time.

C. So it wasn't entirely new to you, it wasn't too difficult.

H. No. It wasn't at all difficult to get used to the idea.

C. Do you feel that you still need to have some kind of a structure, in the sense of having any kind of a reading scheme, are you using your Ginn books at all for that?

H. Not at all, no, I think the only structure I need is my own record keeping, the books that the children have read, so that if I know the child is consistently choosing a book that's too easy, I can try and direct them to more difficult ones, but certainly not with schemes, no.

C. What about – do you use Letterland?

H. Yes, I love it, I enjoy the stories more than the children.

C. Because they're getting to the point now, with you where they're beginning to write independently. I was wondering if shared reading has spinoffs in the areas of writing and spelling, use of dictionaries.

H. With dictionaries, the children are very happy to pick them up, because they're just another book, the big fat yellow dictionaries with lots of pictures in, they often pick them at reading time to look at.

C. Looking at words and the pictures that match them? Oh that's interesting.

H. Yes, so that to pick them up when they're doing their writing is just a natural progression, they're just starting to do it.

C. What about information books, how do they use those?

H. Sometimes they pick them up from the shelves outside, they'll say 'Oh can I have a look at this one?' They'll filter into the classroom that way. We've got a favourite at the moment about dangerous sea creatures, with a marvellous picture of a shark on the front, the pages are falling out, it's been looked at so many times.

C. What *Jaws* has done for teachers! Nearly as popular as dinosaurs now isn't it?

H. Yes!

C. What about... are there any things you'd change about the way you're doing it at the moment?

H. No, not change, I think my own recording of what books the children are reading, if I had extra pairs of hands, I'd add a little bit more, but I think the way I've got it at the moment is efficient use of time.

C. There is a school we've been to where they have a nice system of feedback, they have an exercise book in the bookbag that goes home, and the teacher gives some indication of how the child will share the book, and the parent will write on how it's worked out. I think what I've enjoyed is being able to show parents how they can look out for various strategies developing, noticing when they use picture clues, when they're self-correcting.

H. I think we're very lucky in the sort of parents we've got, they are noticing things like that.

C. And they tell you?

H. Yes.

C. Do you feel it's made the school more comfortable with parents?

H. I feel they take a more active part, certainly.

C. Have you had any problems, any worries about shared reading, any parents who feel they'd rather the old-fashioned methods?

H. Oh no, not at all, Carola's done a very good P.R. job. And in fact it's the opposite, there's this woman who's a supply teacher who comes in a lot, she's so thrilled, because Sally, her daughter, she's just six, she's just finished reading *The Owl Who Was Afraid of the Dark*, and she wants to take *Flat Stanley* home, she's always had an interest in books, I think in a reading scheme system that could so easily have been squashed.

C. Yes, that's right, it's the idea that you can get the child to judge, I mean if they go on choosing books that are too easy, you give them a little nudge, don't you, but the fact is that you're not restricting them to certain levels.

H. And of course with only four classes, there's such freedom of movement, the children feel they can go anywhere to choose a book.

C. What about your silent reading period, how long does that go on for in your class?

H. It depends, from 10 to 20 minutes, it depends on the particular day.

C. Somebody said to us the other day, she found it terribly artificial, she was watching our video. 'It still looks phony to me.' Had it ever struck you?

H. No, it hasn't, not at all, because it comes so naturally to the children, I mean even though mine are only little, they come in after playtime and get a book, and it's not just at silent reading time, it's their natural thing, to pick up a book anytime. I had juniors last year, and one of the main things I miss is that silent reading with the infants isn't silent, and my own reading has fallen off such a lot since I haven't had half an hour with the juniors.

C. Wonderful! Benefits for teachers, as well.

Discussion between C. and E.

C. Can you just explain what you were doing before you came here?

E. When I was teaching before, with top juniors, I was in a school that was rigorously streamed. I was given the B stream class, and we had the 11 plus. There were lots of backward readers. They did marvellously, but the way that we got them to go on was to give them books that they wanted to read. Because they were living near the coast, they were mad on science, mad on birds, seaweed and anemones, that sort of thing. We'd have a project on that, on seabirds and wild animals, and their reading ages nearly doubled. Now that I think of it we were using the same principles as we are now.

C. It seems so obvious, I can't understand why we haven't said it long ago, I always instinctively felt that that was what I wanted to do.

E. I'm sure we've all done it with our own kids at home. If you're a parent you just do it automatically.

C. It's as Liz Waterland said, in the classroom you're trying to be like the good parent. When you came here, what did you notice about the reading? Was it different from other schools?

E. Well I was very struck right away. The first morning when we had silent reading, I was amazed, the children kept coming up and saying, 'It's such a funny book.' and 'Look what's happened here... ' and 'Do you know what he said?'... and then rushing off and sitting down again. They were obviously enjoying their reading very much, A, and B, they were understanding it too. That did strike me straight away.

C.   And you realized that they'd done it for years, they enjoyed it, they felt that books were valuable.

E.   Yes, yes, and you see the two children in my class who don't feel like that have absolutely no backing at home, so the only time they do read is when they sit on my knee, and with having a big class, you can't do it every day.

C.   What can you do about that? Have you any ideas?

E.   Well I'm trying to hear them read very often, and I'm trying to push books their way that they might find interesting. They're both children with behaviour problems, some people might not agree with this but I've had Carola's support to do this, I've given them *Blackberry Farm* books, which are very comforting, and they've absolutely loved them, they can't get enough of them.

C.   *Brambly Hedge*, they might like those, too.

E.   Yes, because they need the emotional security, you need to give them that as well.

C.   Yes, they do. Now what I want to ask you is how often do they change their books, how often do they take books home, and do you have any parents helping?

E.   Helping with the reading, you mean? Yes we have parents in every week and they hear more or less every child read, and the welfare helpers, too, and the children take their books home, but not every parent hears their child every night, as you would expect, and of course as you would expect, the bad readers, it's their parents who openly admit they hardly hear them read at all.

C.   Do you think there's any way round that, or do you think it's inevitable?

E.   I think it's inevitable, they don't see it as a priority at all. You see, in a way, life to them is the priority, they've got so much to cope with at home, that whether the child is doing his 'homework' or not, which is the way they see it, that's the least of their worries.

C.   It's interesting, though, I've been doing some research into this, there really are only about 2 per cent of parents who won't help, if you get outside the school, into their areas so to speak. If they've had a bad experience of school themselves as a child, they see teachers in a certain way. Of course this argues time for home visits and we can't do that, we have to make the best of it, but there's no doubt about it, a lot more parents would be prepared, and are prepared, and are quite anxious for their children to be happy and do well and to learn to read, but it's getting to them and talking to them in their own homes. At present we don't have time to do that.

E.   I can understand that.

C.   The other thing I was going to ask you, one of my concerns is, when children start internalizing reading, we sometimes assume that they know it, and we don't need to do an awful lot more from then on, and there's some evidence to show that their vocabulary and understanding of the text goes down, so that if they're poor or mediocre readers, by the time they're 13, they're actually reading worse than when they were 9, have you any ideas about this?

E. Yes, well to keep that interest going, maybe we need to look at our own role again, sometimes I think we do a lot of work in the primary school which is then repeated in the secondary school, we do it all across the curriculum, don't we, I mean in Science and so on. Maybe we should have a reading time every day, as we do here, if you actually timetable for reading, and think to yourself, this is the time when I look at the ones with reading difficulties, otherwise, by the time they get to the top juniors, we think the only ones we need to look at are the ones who are having a lot of problems.

C. Are there any other spinoffs, apart from the reading, in using this method?

E. Oh yes I think so, apart from the fact that they are very excited by reading, and the obvious stimulation, there's the spelling.

C. It's good is it?

E. Oh yes, the people who are good readers are also good spellers. It isn't always the case is it?

C. No, no.

E. I've noticed that they are really good spellers.

C. They've done Letterland haven't they?

E. I don't know that system.

C. There is quite a big phonic input in the infants in this school which other schools who do shared reading don't have. It would be interesting to compare this with the next school, where they don't have this system. What about writing?

E. No I don't think it's made any difference, but I haven't been here long enough, I don't think it's really improved their punctuation.

C. And that's something that they still haven't mastered when they get to your class?

E. Well I've got a big age range, from 6 to 8, obviously the 8-year-olds are coping with it, maybe it's one of those things that depends on maturity.

C. One thing about punctuation is, reading aloud helps with it, so that's something I would do more about with the juniors in our school.

E. Letting them read aloud?

C. Yes, because then you can see why we need punctuation.

E. Yes but then you see, bad readers don't punctuate their reading well.

C. But I've had much less of that 'barking at print' with shared reading. Those two little infants that read to me this morning, they've been doing shared reading from the word go, they read to me with considerable expression.

E. None of the Da Da Da, the chant!

C. So if they read aloud to me in the juniors, it might help, don't you think?

The next thing we're looking at with the Literacy Committee is writing. How does it affect their writing?

E. Well let's see – for the younger ones, it's such a lot for them to cope with, first of all they have to marshall their thoughts, you have to do that before you begin to write, then they have to put a stopper on it and say that's enough, then they have to think about, does that make sense, before they write it down, think of the spelling, and they have to be neat, and they have to make the letters properly. Quite frankly, I'm not surprised if at 7 they can't do all that.

C. No. I've just been looking at some books on writing, schools where the teachers let children try, without any instruction at all, they've surrounded them with writing, but they've let them come to it.

E. A sort of apprenticeship approach to writing.

C. Yes, that's it!

Discussion between C. and two children who have had some reading difficulties

C. Can you tell me what you were reading this morning in the silent period?

A. Roald Dahl's *Boy*. Roald Dahl's my favourite author.

C. I wonder, have they made *Boy* into a film yet?

A. No, anyway I'd rather read a book.

C. Why, what's nice about reading a book?

A. Well, anyone can go out and see a film. When I'm reading I see the words in my head, but sometimes they get muddled up.

C. What's *Boy* about?

A. It's about Roald Dahl when he was little. He's Norwegian, and he's got quite a lot of brothers and sisters. He had a father, and the father's best daughter died, and the father was so sad that he died as well. And he had to go to school, and there's this awful lady in the sweet shop. And she's always going on about his grubby hands. So they went to get their own back on her, and there's a secret place where they keep all the gobstoppers and sweets, it's a loose floorboard in school. One day they found a dead mouse, so they went along to the shop, and they put the dead mouse into the gobstopper bowl, and the next morning they came back and there was smashed glass all over the floor, and gobstoppers, and a dead mouse in the middle of it, and the next day, she, Mrs Cratchit came to school and his Mum got really cross and went to school and talked to the head master and said she didn't want him caned, so she sent him to another school, and that's where I've got to.

C. What do you think about the idea of caning?

A. It's horrible.

C. No way to treat people is it? Now have you read any other Roald Dahl books?

A   *The Witches, The Twits, The Magic Finger, Charlie and the Chocolate Factory, The Glass Elevator,* I've read most of them.

C.   Tell me what you like about them, A.

A.   He's always writing about horrid old ladies, and I like the descriptions and things.

C.   I wonder if you've noticed that, there is always a horrid old lady in his stories. *James and the Giant Peach* was the first one I read, with the two horrid aunties.

A.   I haven't read that one yet, but I want to.

C.   And he also has quite a lot of children in his stories.

A.   Yes, some nice and some absolutely horrible. Some are very clever.

C.   So you like the characters of the people in his books.

A.   Yes, especially where he gets the drawings done by Quentin Blake.

C.   Oh so do I, he's the perfect illustrator, I think *The Witches* is particularly good. But there's something else, what about his actual stories? What we call the plot.

A.   I think they're really good.

C.   He's certainly a very original writer isn't he?

A.   He usually has a nice lady in as well.

C.   Now then, J. What have you been reading?

J.   I've been reading *A Hundred and One Dalmatians*. I liked it better than the film.

C.   Why is that?

J.   Well the book gives you more information.

C.   What did you specially like?

J.   I like the bit where Mrs Pongo and Mrs ? go in the carriage together which is a bit of a squeeze, she's got 50 puppies.

C.   Do you think it's a likely story?

J.   No.

C.   Why not?

J.   I'm not sure.

C.   What do you know about dogs having puppies, do you know much about it?

J.   Well my dog had six puppies, and Shadow, who we had to get rid of, she had seven.

C.   Yes, seven, so a hundred and one.

J.   Is a lot!

C.   Now! An interesting thing, A. was talking about the horrid lady in *Boy*, what about *A Hundred and One Dalmatians*?

J.   I can't remember her first name, Devil, oh yes Cruella Deville.

C.   And if you look at the word, it's really...

J.   Devil!

C.   So that's another horrid lady in a book, I wonder if horrid ladies are worse than horrid men? Are there any horrid men in books that you find really frightening?

J.   There's a sort of ogre, in a fairytale book. There's one in a book about ghosts.

C.   What about horrid children?

J.   This book I read the other day had some in.

C.   Oh is that the *Nursery Crimes* book?

J.   Yes and then there's *My Naughty Little Sister*.

C.   Where do you like to be when you're reading, what's your best place for reading?

A.   Somewhere warm, and comfortable, in my bedroom.

C.   And what about you J.?

J.   I can read in my bedroom, too.

C.   Have you got plenty of books of your own at home?

A.   Yes, but the trouble is with that, once you've read them, there's nothing else you can do with them except read them again.

C.   Yes, well I have favourite books I read more than once. And how often do you change books that you borrow from school?

A.   Well we don't have much of a library here now. We have little stickers on the book, and if you're good at reading, you can have, say, black.

C.   You can take home what you like, can you? Or does the teacher tell you what to take home?

A.   Well you pick the book and the teacher says, 'That's alright', then you can take it home.

C.   How does it work, do you have to sign something, take a ticket out?

J.   You've got this blue book, to say what you've been reading, and when you've finished you've got to write a little bit about it.

C.   And how easy is that?

J.   Fairly easy.

C.   How long does it have to be, or can you write as much as you like?

J.   Well there's not many lines, so it's what you can get on the page.

C.   Now tell me about reading in this school, how does it work, I'm very interested.

J.   Well we have 15-minutes silent reading, and some sit out in the library area, or you sit on the mat in the classroom or at tables.

C.   Who decides who sits in the library?

J.   The teacher.

C.   Where's the quietest?

J.   Out here in the library, or in the hall.

A.   And then we read at night, we read at home.

C.   So that gives you plenty of practice, doesn't it? And do you two both read inside your head now?

A.
J.   } Oh yes.

C.   Do you ever do any reading out loud?

A.   Well I read to my sister sometimes. And she reads to me.

C. Yes, it's a good idea to read to somebody younger, you can practise acting, like, well, putting on the witchy voice.

A. My old teacher, she was terribly good at telling stories. You know the one, *Bremen, Musicians of Bremen*, well at the end of it, some of us would do the cockroaches, some of us would do the cat, we'd all make a horrible noise.

C. Great, a good way of telling a story. What about poetry, do you read much in class?

A. I like kind of funny poetry, otherwise it's rather long.

J. I like little short ones.

C. Yes, do you know Spike Milligan, Roger McGough?

A. My favourite one is the one about the baboon that flew to the sun. He goes past something or other at one.

A. Have you heard of *Nursery Crimes* or something?

C. What's that?

A. It's over there, it was on Swop Shop, chap with a big beard, he writes lots of children's poems. Its not Roald Dahl, I've read most of his books.

Discussion between C. and two good readers, aged 9

C. Well you start, P., who's your favourite author?

P. C.S. Lewis. I've got all the Narnia books at home.

C. Which one did you like best?

P. *The Lion, the Witch and the Wardrobe.* I didn't have the first edition, so I got the second edition.

C. That's a wonderful story, full of ideas, I enjoyed that one. What did you feel when you were reading it, could you see things in your head?

P. Yes, my father read it to me, and I pictured it in my head, as they were walking through the water into the land of Narnia.

C. Have you ever seen the play of it?

M. We went with the school.

C. How did you feel about that?

P. It was good. It was a bit muddling though, they kind of went to one bit, which was meant to be at the same time as they were at home, one minute they were in the house, and the next minute they were in Narnia.

C. So that was a bit difficult. I see. Did they actually walk through the wardrobe in it? How did they do it?

P. Well the stage went black and then they put a different set on.

C. So you do know how it worked then? You didn't think it was magic? I expect some of the little ones did. Somebody told me it was a very good show. Did it spoil the book for you at all?

M. No. You see I'd read it before.

C. What kind of pictures would you have in your head if you read it again now?

M. Same as last time.

P.   I suppose it might change a bit. I might think of it in more detail because I'd be reading it for the second time.

C.   Yes, you would, wouldn't you. Now, M. what about you, who's your favourite author?

M.   Diana Wynne-Jones. I like *The Eight Days of Luke.*

C.   Yes, it's terrific. I'll tell you a strange thing about that. I hadn't read that book when I was little, because it hadn't been written. So when I was teaching, Mrs G. your head said to me 'Have you read this book? It's really super.' Well, as soon as I'd read it I had to get all her other books, I enjoyed it so much. You see, it's a good book for grown-ups as well. That's the thing about a really good book, anyone can enjoy it whatever age they are. Can you describe the plot to me, so I can listen to the way it came across to you?

M.   Well there's this boy, David, who has horrid relatives, they're not very nice. He wants to put a curse on them. He says all the funny words he can think of, and suddenly this wall falls down and all these snakes come out, and Luke appears.

C.   Tell me about Luke.

M.   He's this boy who says he's been in prison underground, he's really a god called Loki. David doesn't find that out till the end. Then some strange people come. Well, all the Viking gods come, Woden.

C.   The man with the raven on his shoulder.

M.   Yes, there were two ravens in the story.

C.   Did you know about the old Norse gods before you read the story?

M.   Yes, because we went to York.

C.   Good, because I think you'd miss an awful lot of that book if you didn't know those old stories.

P. }
M. } Yes, you wouldn't know what the book was on about.

C.   Absolutely. I felt when I read it, 'Good Heavens, this is about Woden and Thor'. Did you know there's a very famous series of operas about those Norse gods, I went to see one last year, Woden had the big hat, and the patch over one eye, and the raven, and he wanders the world, finding out what people are up to. Now what did you feel about the little boy David in the book?

P.   I felt sorry for him, and Astrid his cousin was always being picked on and she stuck up for him and in the end the police found out that the relatives had been using David's money.

C.   Yes. David was a very angry boy, wasn't he? Did you understand that his anger released Loki from his prison?

P.   Yes, I did in the end.

C.   What else did you read by her, M.?

M.   *Archer's Goon. The Ogre Downstairs.*

C.   *The Power of Three?*

M.   I started that but I didn't like it. Oh I know *The Magicians of Caprona.*

C. What other authors do you like?

P. ⎫
M. ⎭ Roald Dahl.

C. What makes his books so special?

P. They're exciting, he kind of chooses them for his daughter or someone. Like in the BFG, he's the giant and she's the little girl.

C. What do you think he does with his stories to get your interest?

P. He kind of takes them from real life and changes them.

M. Yes he turns them into magical things.

C. Fantasy?

M. Yes. Like the cucumbers, you know.

C. Have you read *Danny the Champion of the World*? The children in my school love it because we're a country school.

P. Yes and he lives in a caravan.

C. What about the baddies and the goodies in his books?

P. There's the Twits, the Witches, the aunties in *James and the Giant Peach*.

M. All them rich kind of kids in *Charlie and the Chocolate Factory*.

P. The Fat boy.

M. That was Mick, the TV boy.

C. Can you think of any other book with horrid children in?

M. Cinderella.

P. They're not children.

C. I wonder if we can find a clue as to why children like Roald Dahl so much?

P. Well he kind of takes a really innocent child and then there's bullies.

C. He seems to remember what it feels like to be bullied. And he has some horrible grown-ups too.

M. Well like in *A Hundred and One Dalmatians* there's Cruella Deville.

P. He expresses his feelings in his books.

C. Did you know a lot of grown-ups aren't too keen on Roald Dahl books? They feel they're not terribly nice.

P. I expect children like them because the parents don't like adults being baddies.

M. And the children are OK. [Laughter]

C. Now I wonder where you like to read? P?

P. Oh just on my bed.

C. Why's that?

P. Because it's quiet and there aren't any people there.

C. What would it be like if you were reading in the living room?

M. Oh my sister would be there.

P. Dad and Mum would be coming in and out the door, and the telly would be on.

C. Yes I understand, what about in school?

M. We can either sit in there [pointing to classroom], or out here. We have to be really silent. Except for A.W.

C. There's always somebody, isn't there?

P. Yes. We kind of have a privilege of sitting out here.

C. Who decides?

M. Teachers.

C. And the teachers read as well, in silent reading? How long do you get?

M. Twenty minutes, but sometimes we have longer.

C. Do you get a story read to you at the end of the afternoon?

P. Not always. *The Eight Days of Luke* and *Archer's Goon* were read to us by Mrs G.

P. We've just started *Elidor* by Alan Garner. About the unicorn and the children going into another world. They have swords and things in the other world, but when they're in the proper world, the swords are just bits of wood.

C. Some of his later books are really difficult, because his ideas are so difficult, but they're well worth it. What else have you read?

M. *The Weirdstone of Brisingamen.*

C. Yes, it's a hard name to say. That's the one about Cheshire isn't it? Now what about bad books, can you tell a really phony book when you read it?

M. Oh yes Enid Blyton, I used to read loads of them.

C. Doesn't your taste change as you get older? I used to love the *Adventure* books when I was about 7, younger than you two.

P. I've read *The Castle of Adventure*. I used to like those *Little Bod* stories.

M. Oh no! Well I liked *Miffy at the Seaside*. I used to love that.

P. I used to be mad on *Bod*, now I look at them and think 'How come I was such a twit as to read that?'

C. Have you come across any books for your age now that you don't like?

P. I don't like really dragged out stories. Kind of... you don't get any action in it.

M. It just sort of carries on and on, the same thing.

C. So what are you after?

P. Good action, like in *Goodnight Mr Tom*.

C. I haven't read that yet, don't tell me too much about it.

M. It's great, Nadine Simmons has read it 15 times.

C. Do you like reading the same book over and over again?

M. Sometimes. I'm just going to start reading *Back Home* again.

C. What about poetry?

P. *The Nursery Crimes* one.

C. By Michael Rosen?

P. Yes.

C. Sometimes teachers just read funny poems to children, we're a bit afraid to read serious poems. The eight-year-olds I teach are just starting on what we call narrative poems, story poems with me, they love them. Reading poetry about moods and the seasons are more difficult, that's where you need to read aloud.

Headteacher   What do you think about the T. S. Eliot poems we're doing now?

P.   Great they're good. We haven't done the *Naming of Cats* yet.

C.   He was a very famous poet, of course, who wrote some very beautiful serious poems you'll be able to read when you're older. Which of the cat poems do you like best?

M.   Oh, McCavity.

P.   I like them all, and I like the music.

M.   Yes, *Memory* is my favourite.

P.   Yes.

CHAPTER 6

Monitoring progress

The use of traditional methods of teaching reading has meant that it has always been relatively simple for both teachers and parents to be immediately aware of the level of a child's reading ability. The 'whole story' approach means that assessment of reading development needs to be evaluated in quite a different way, once the hierarchical level of reading schemes has been removed.

Before examining possible methods of assessment, we need to reflect on why we need to do this, and who we are doing it for. While we have been evaluating the practice of shared reading in this division, it has been most illuminating to discover the diversification in attitudes to assessment and its purposes. Many heads rely on the professional judgement of their staff, carrying out the minimum of formal testing. They consider that frequent testing is an unnecessary waste of time, and that this is only useful when children are having specific reading difficulties or as a regular method of monitoring the school's reading standards (e.g. on transfer from infant to junior school). At the other extreme we found schools where formal, diagnostic tests were given to every child at least twice a year.

Certainly the LEA needs to monitor the standards of education in its schools, and regular screening at say 7, 11, and 15 will give a complete picture of the level of ability in basic subject areas. Heads and teachers need to be informed of the individual progress of each pupil, particularly at times of transfer to a new class or school. Parents, too, have the right to be aware of the current ability level of their child. Above all we owe it to the children to provide a method which charts individual reading development, provides a comprehensive profile of ability level and highlights any areas of difficulty. Clearly any LEA screening is carried out using a standardized testing procedure. Individual schools, however, need to develop their own methods of assessment, giving teachers and parents a profile which includes qualitative judgements rather than merely a 'reading age' figure.

Ideally, we consider that each child should have an ongoing reading profile, which covers the whole primary school stage. In drawing up our own such profile we used the following criteria:

1. It needed to be simple to administer; any tests should be usable as a group activity, in the familiarity of the classroom.
2. Scoring methods should be straightforward, and progress be simple to chart and read from a flow chart.
3. Any test used should have visual appeal to a child.
4. Cost should not be prohibitive.
5. It should consist of two strands:
   (a) a validated, standardized reading test for vocabulary, comprehension, speed and accuracy;
   (b) a qualitative, continuous assessment by the class teacher showing the development of reading behaviour.

Reading tests

We examined a number of standardized reading tests. Many were perfectly adequate for testing individual children, particularly for diagnostic assessment (e.g. Hunter-Grundin and Neale's *Analysis*). Few tests satisfied our criteria 1–4, particularly for use with Infant classes. The most suitable tests for children which satisfied our criteria, were Young's, The Hertfordshire Reading Test and Daniels and Diack (though only the Young test was able to be administered on a group basis). Apart from the Young test, all the tests we considered appeared rather dated or dull.

Continuous assessment

The reading profiles (below) include all the stages of reading development which we consider to be necessary for the child to progress from the pre-reading stage to that of the independent reader. Each stage has a space for the class teacher to record dates and comments, so that the areas of difficulty can readily be identified and appropriate action taken.

A reading profile

We suggest that if each child is given a standardized reading test at the end of each primary school year (though not necessarily at the reception/middle infant stage) this can then be recorded on their reading profile. Then a complete record of competence is always available. On the reverse of the profile there is a list of books appropriate to that stage, to which can be added a list of books read by the child. Obviously more diagnostic testing may be required when a child fails to move through a certain stage.

Shared reading is very much in its infancy in North Hertfordshire, so that, at this stage, no longitudinal surveys have been possible. Any general rather than individual monitoring has to be qualitative rather than quantitive.

One local head, whose infant school introduced shared reading two years ago, found that on transfer to junior school, on average, each child was reading 10 months ahead of his chronological age, when Young's test was used. A village school head has observed that, after using shared reading for three years, she no longer encountered any non-readers and the children were ready to move into secondary education.

With the lack of data available so far, our monitoring of shared reading has produced comments such as 'all the children are reading more confidently' or 'his class show a real awareness of critical skills'. Some data, however, is available from other areas where parental involvement has been established for some time. The Haringey project was closely monitored by Jenny Hewison over a total period of three years (1976–9). Here, directed by Professor Jack Tizard, six of the borough's schools had the reading progress of their top infant classes evaluated. Two classes took books home to read to parents, two classes received extra help at school and two more acted as control groups. Reading performance, tested before the project, was higher two years later in the classes with parental involvement. One year later these same children were still ahead of the control group, with half of the children who had received parent help reading at or above their chronological age level. By comparison, one-fifth of the control group were at this level. In an area where reading standards had been consistently below the national average, this was seen as showing a significant improvement. Results showed too, that less children produced results at the weakest level of the NFER test used (only 6 per cent were below a score of 84, where parents were involved compared with 17 per cent at this level in the control group).

The progress of the children receiving remedial help in school was also monitored and it was found that they made less progress than those supported by parents. The study concluded, 'The findings of the present study suggest that staffing resources at present allocated by LEA's for remedial work in primary schools might be better employed, at least in part, in organizing contact and collaboration between class teachers and parents – all parents, before failure is manifest for some children – on specific, practical teaching matters, and that this might prevent many children from falling behind with their reading in the first place' (Tizard *et al.* 1982).

Similar results were recorded over a four-year period in Jackson's and Hannon's evaluation of the Belfield Reading Project (1981). In addition Topping and McKnight conclude that the longer parents are involved, then the greater are the gains in total reading age improvement (1984). In a research document to be published soon by the Open University Press, Chapman has found that a third of the 1500 children surveyed made no progress in their reading once they left primary school. Certainly our local observations have led us to the conclusion that many junior schools are failing to cater for continued fluency in reading, once a certain level of competency has been achieved. We feel that if more junior schools would be willing to involve parents, then reading development is more likely to continue, as Topping suggests.

Many parents, who have been involved in the early stages of their child's reading, are only too willing to continue into the junior school stage. More junior schools should be willing to work together with such parents so that reading momentum is maintained. An enjoyment of books is being fostered at infant level and must be nurtured throughout the junior stage and beyond, so that the end product is a generation of book-loving young adults. It is only by meticulous monitorings of both school and individual that we can ensure that more children really are developing into fluent and avid readers.

The Stubbs/Davis Reading Profile

Many teachers have asked us for a simple method of recording reading progress. We offer this profile, which is designed to record teachers' observations of the child's reading development from pre-reading behaviour to fluent reading for enjoyment and meaning. We have included the development of study skills and the growth of recognition of the style and purpose of text. We also felt it was necessary to record some aspects of language development and writing because they are closely linked with reading development.

We hope teachers will use this profile to record and date the gradual progress of the child at each stage, so we have made space for more than one entry in each box. There is room, too, for teachers to make a brief note of any particular strategies they use for the child who needs extra help. On the back of each sheet we have listed books which we think children should be able to read as they progress through each stage. We took these books from Moon's *Individualised Reading* booklist. We suggest that teachers may prefer to make their own list from the books they use in their classrooms. We have included some reading scheme books and several storybooks so that the child has plenty of choice. We also felt that it is important to record the child's own favourite books at each stage.

The concepts we have used are based on the system used by Liz Waterland and on our own observations. There are two concepts which require further explanation. The third box in Stage 2 records the link between growing confidence in reading and play. We have noticed that children who are beginning to enjoy reading like to act out their new experiences. They pretend to read to their dolls, organize 'libraries' and 'schools' with their friends, and fold pieces of paper to make 'books'. This is not book-making directed by the teacher, but a play activity initiated by the child. The 'books' will have drawings and random letters and words written in them, and the child may ask an adult for help with the writing of a name or phrase.

In the sixth box in Stage 2 we highlight a strategy used by adults and children alike when confronted by a difficult piece of text. We sometimes repeat aloud a sentence or phrase using different emphasis and inflection several times if we are unsure of the meaning of the words. This attention to the rhythm of the prose is a strategy we have noticed children using, sometimes when they are reading aloud to an adult, or when they are reading silently, just beginning to internalize their reading.

We have not attempted to tie the four stages to chronological age, although we expect the normal child to have reached Stage 4 on transition from junior to secondary school. We decided not to number each box, because the children develop reading skills in many ways. We felt that the teacher's own dated observations were a better indication of progress than an artificially imposed hierarchy.

Copies of the Reading Profile may be obtained from ATP (Education) Ltd, Grove Chambers, Nightingale Road, Hitchin, Herts. Price £1.50 for photo-copying for individual use in school.

Stubbs/Davis Reading Profile

Name of child:

Stage 1

Age at start of record:

School:

Is able to listen to story. Is aware of plot and pictures. Has favourites. Enjoys choosing books with adult help. Likes visiting library or bookshop.	

Is eager to share books. Knows how a book works, e.g. gets it right way up, turns pages, opens book at beginning.	

Behaves like a reader. Browses, looks at pictures, talks about books, is beginning to discriminate. Can read story through pictures.	

Shows interest in text. Knows that story is told in text. Points to own name letter. May recognize individual words.	

Moves finger underneath words or follows with eyes while adult reads, or when browsing. Recites story from memory.	

Begins to repeat words of well-known book, looking at text. Joins in with adult reader. Fills in missing word.	

© R. Stubbs, C. Davis, 1987.

65

Suggestions for books appreciated at stage 1.	Child's own favourites
Ahlberg, A. *Each Peach, Pear, Plum.* Campbell, R. *Dear Zoo.* Carle, E. *The Very Hungry Caterpillar.* Hill, E. *Where's Spot?* Hutchins, P. *Rosie's Walk.* Watanabe, S. *How Do I Put it On?* Bruna books. Storychest Big Books. Tiddlywinks. Get Ready Books.	

Stubbs/Davis Reading Profile **Stage 2**

Name of child:

Age at start of record:

School:

Is beginning to predict. Has a fund of well-known favourite stories. Enjoys choosing books with adult help.	

Is confident in talking about books and sharing them with others. Is beginning to develop study skills, e.g. uses simple dictionary.	

Tries to write own stories and makes 'little books' independently. Plays 'libraries' and 'schools'.	

Understands the meaning of 'letter', 'word' and 'sentence'. Is aware of the shape and length of words. Notices punctuation.	

Is beginning to use precise strategies, e.g. context and picture clues. Is using initial letter sounds.	

When reading aloud uses the rhythm of the prose to understand text, and reads aloud to correct meaning. Attempts independent reading of known text.	

© R. Stubbs, C. Davis, 1987.

67

Suggestions for books appreciated at stage 2.	Child's own favourites
Ahlberg, A. *Happy Families* series. Burningham, J. *Would you Rather?* *Mr Gumpy's Outing.* Dodd, L. *Hairy McClary.* Dr Seuss *The Cat in the Hat* (and others). Hutchins, P. *Titch.* Nicoll, H. *Meg and Mog.* Storychest Rhymes and Plays. Ready Set Go. Bangers and Mash 1–6 1,2,3 and away Introductory Books. Breakthrough to Literacy Yellow and Red Levels.	

Stubbs/Davis Reading Profile   **Stage 3**

Name of child: Age at start of record: School:

Is reading simple unknown text without adult help. Uses previous experience to analyse new words.	

Is attempting more difficult unknown text still with adult help. Is willing to attempt difficult text alone.	

Is able to read aloud with expression and retells stories in own words. Is self-correcting.	

Is internalizing text. Is beginning to read independently for instruction and information from several sources.	

Discriminates between different types of text, appreciates poetry, enjoys variety of style, plot and character.	

Is using variety of decoding strategies, e.g. phonic blending, recognition of morphemes. Enjoys form and function of words for their own sake.	

© R. Stubbs, C. Davis, 1987.

Suggestions for books appreciated at stage 3.	Child's own favourites

Biro, V. *Gumdrop*.
Browne, A. *Gorilla*.
Dahl, R. *Fantastic Mr Fox*.
Hughes, S. *Alfie's Feet*.
    Dogger.
Lobel, A. *Frog and Toad Stories*.
    Mouse Tales.
Bangers and Mash 7–12
Ginn Fairy Stories.
Collections of poems, riddles and fairy stories.	

Stubbs/Davis Reading Profile   **Stage 4**

Name of child:

Age at start of record:

School:

Is able to tell stories using own storytelling language. Retells own favourites, selecting key elements of plot and character.	

Can review books, with clear idea of preferences and reasons for them. Knows work of individual authors.	

Uses library independently, belongs to school book club. Likes to have books as presents. Enjoys private reading.	

Is able to skim text and scan for required information.	

Is developing critical skills. Understands bias. Can relay information with awareness of writer's point of view.	

Is refining study skills, e.g. use of index, catalogue, dictionary, encyclopaedia.	

© R. Stubbs, C. Davis, 1987.

71

Suggestions for books appreciated at stage 4.	Child's own favourites
Blume, J. *Blubber.* Dahl, R. *Danny, the Champion of the World.* Lewis, C.S. *Narnia* books. Murphy, J. *The Worst Witch.* Mark, J. *Thunder and Lightnings.* Naughton, B. *The Goalkeeper's Revenge.* Pearce, P. *The Battle of Bubble and Squeak.* Wynne-Jones, D. *The Power of Three.* White, E. *Charlotte's Web.* Information books, puzzle books, books of narrative poetry.	

CHAPTER 7

Foreseeing the problems

We are aware that our enthusiasm for shared reading sometimes makes it seem easier than it is. The relaxed and friendly atmosphere, with parents, teachers and children working together is not achieved without time and care. If we are to see parents and teachers as partners, we may have to make a radical change in our attitudes to each other. There may be pitfalls along the way! In this chapter, we would like to look at some of the problems we have encountered, in the hope that you may be able to avoid them or know how to deal with them when they arise. Of necessity, our account is anecdotal, but these are real problems which have come up in our own schools.

There are two main areas of difficulty. The organizational problems have been discussed in Chapter 4. We emphasize again that you need time and a lot of hard work if you are going to succeed in organizing your scheme so that you have a good supply of books and a foolproof method of changing them. We have found teachers to be adaptable and inventive in their approach to the practical problems. The hard part of adopting a scheme with parental involvement is dealing with our own worries and making sure that parents too are convinced of the value of shared reading. The schools we have visited have differed widely in size and catchment area, but the personal problems we have encountered were remarkably similar. We have tried to analyse them in the hope of providing some pointers towards solving them. The characters we met appeared so often that we felt they could appear in a play. Do they sound familiar to you? The 'pushy' parent, the 'invisible' parent, the reluctant colleague, the indifferent headteacher and the staff-room politician all had something to tell us about our own attitudes and our reluctance to make changes. Some of these characters faded away like ghosts when approached with confidence, while some required the diplomacy of an ambassador. If you are reading this book, you may well be interested in shared reading already, and may already be enthusiastic about parental involvement. If so you are one of the lucky ones. There are many people who find innovation frightening, or who are anxious at being asked to add yet another burden to their load. We know how much we have gained, we have been delighted to see children growing in confidence in their reading, we have made friends with parents, discovered a depth of interest and support from them that we never suspected, and we have found that we teach reading now with enthusiasm and success. It has taken us a long time to get to this point. We would like to look first at the sort of problems you may come across with parents.

Problems with parents

Where do you begin? If you already have a flourishing PTA, and have parents helping in school with cooking, sport and craft work, you have a head start. But you probably have an élite. We are grateful to that small and much valued band of parents who offer their services willingly, but we would like all parents to be involved. We think it is important to talk to all the parents, to visit them at home if necessary, to make sure that each child in your class has a caring adult prepared to help with reading at home on a daily basis. Some parents seem almost too eager. We suspect their motives and worry that they will besiege us with requests for evidence of progress, going through children's desks, making invidious comparisons and getting in our hair. These are the parents we frequently call 'pushy'. They wonder whether state education is failing their children, they hanker for the old grammar school education, wonder why 'you don't teach tables any more', they ask for homework and want you to pay more attention to spelling and punctuation.

If you work in a village school, or in an area with expensive housing, you will recognize these parents, we feel sure. They believe their child is intelligent, they have provided all the right educational toys and books, and they ask why their child does not talk about what goes on in school or bring any books home. Such parents often like the idea of a reading scheme with its obvious ladder of progression. They will happily use flashcards at home, or help their child learn 10 spellings a week, and they know that they are more 'successful', prosperous and intelligent than you are. They are keenly aware of the educational status of schools in the locality, and they hate teachers taking industrial action. We have seen rather too much of them lately, and we think that they may be the most likely cause of a headteacher's reluctance to introduce parental involvement in school. What do we really mean by a 'pushy' parent? It is possible to think instead of a parent who wants the best for his child? Isn't that exactly what teachers are like about their own children? Oh, we know the jargon better, we know what to look out for in the modern classroom, but we too have doubts about our child's school if we are not made to feel welcome, and have no idea what goes on during the day. Some of us are a little afraid of adverse criticism from articulate parents who may well write letters to the governing body. We know that they may decide to take their children away and turn to the private sector, and this can be very disheartening when we work hard to give each child in our care the very best teaching we have to offer. We tend to hide behind 'professionalism' like doctors or lawyers, keeping our classroom doors firmly shut.

We suggest that we will do more to restore parents' confidence if we break down the barriers by talking to parents, than if we deny them their place in their child's education. Shared reading is a wonderful way to begin co-operating with parents, and we have found that the understanding it generates about reading spreads to other areas of the curriculum, and parents become more supportive of the school. The parent who is anxious to see progress will need reassurance that you are working with them because you believe that it is good educational practice. She will need to know that reading taught by using 'real' books instead of reading scheme books is not just the latest fad. Sometimes the anxiety of parents takes the form of aggressive refusal to listen to your point of view. It is helpful to be able to show parents the evidence that shared reading works.

We think it is a good idea to have a bookshelf for parents, and we offer, at the end of this chapter, a booklist we think suitable. Not all parents want to read up the subject, but if they do, we think they will find these books helpful. We encourage them to read several books to get a balanced picture. We had no idea how much parents wanted to understand what we were doing until we introduced shared reading at a coffee morning and showed parents copies of Waterland's *Read With Me*. We explained rather apologetically that it was written for teachers, but the books were snapped up, and many parents came back to ask if we had any other suggestions, which led us to compile the booklist. Parents were glad of the opportunity to do some work themselves, while understanding that reading is far more complex than they had imagined.

Once they understood that their part in the process was relatively simple, and that there was no need for them to sound out words or worry about levels of difficulty in the text of a book, they began to enjoy helping. The most important message we felt we should convey to them was that there are many strategies used by good readers, all of them part of 'a patterning of complex behaviour' as Clay describes it. One mother had concentrated on phonics with her six-year-old, who had become less and less enthusiastic about reading. She knew that she had conveyed her anxieties to the child. We encouraged her to read to him for a while, and simply enjoy a bedtime story.

After we had talked over the reading process together, she began to share books with him, with a lot of support from the teacher. 'It's so easy, doing it this way', she said, 'I thought it was terribly technical and I didn't really believe that this sharing business would work. It was quite hard for me to take the pressure off at first, I really had to bite my tongue when he forgot a word he should have known. Now he's reading to his little brother and we're all enjoying it so much more.' This parent needed to express her anxieties and wanted a lot of reassurance that she hadn't destroyed her child's confidence completely. It's asking a lot of a busy teacher to take so much time with one parent, but everyone benefited from the experience. 'Pushy' parents take a while to understand that pressure is counter productive for a child who is already anxious, and that competition is for parents rather than for children. If you can persuade them to try shared reading, and reassure them that you have a good monitoring system, the results within a few months will be ample justification of your methods.

The invisible parent

How much easier it is to consider the 'invisible' parents! We can, if we like, ignore them, and it is tempting to make disparaging remarks to the effect that they are not interested in their child's education. We may have already given time and effort in attempting to support them, but feel that our efforts have been wasted. It is not easy for us to understand or sympathize with someone who never responds to our written communications, who never comes to Parents' Evenings, or attends school functions. Some of us have said, 'But our parents don't want to be involved, they have too many problems, they can't read, she's a battered wife, he doesn't speak English, they both work, they hated school themselves, they think it's our job to teach, they just don't want to know.' If we begin to look at our own prejudices, we can see that we present, as teachers, a middle-class image which sets us apart from some of the families we work with.

Before we decide that parental involvement is a non-starter in our particular school, it would be as well to look at the evidence. Many of the projects which proved the value of home/school liaison took place over many years in areas where communication between home and school had been difficult, and where assumptions had been made about parents' views of education and level of language development which were not borne out in practice.

The conclusion of the Haringey research team was that 'in inner-city multi-racial schools, it is both feasible and practicable to involve nearly all parents in formal educational activities with infant and first-year junior children, even if the parents are non-literate or largely non-English speaking'. Professor Tizard, who set up the project said, 'We cannot emphasize strongly enough the love, pride and interest that all the parents in the sample showed towards their children.' Parents in Sheffield who lived in an area where housing was poor and conditions were drab, were found to provide a rich language environment for their children, and were eager to take part in a shared reading project. Some families will always be better informed and more self-sufficient than others, but the gap in language provision and interest in the child's development is not nearly as wide as many teachers assume.

Children are part of their home community, and the experience they bring to school from that community is one that we should value. If parents seem to be unwilling to be involved in their child's schooling, we must look to our own attitudes and ways of communicating. Are we approaching parents in a way that makes them feel diminished? Do we truly value their contribution to their child's growth? We have never yet met a parent who did not want their child to read. It is what they tell their children they go to school for. Even when they are prepared to acknowledge their own lack of interest or skill, they hope their children will manage better. 'I want to give them what I never had', said one mother taking part in a reading course in Leicestershire.

Shared reading is something all parents can do with very little formal training, and it may well be that many of them are already doing it if we took the trouble to ask. If we can give parents pride in what they have already taught their children, they will be more likely to want to work with us. There is no substitute for personal contact with 'invisible' parents, and home visits are more likely to be successful than invitations into the classroom at first. If parents have unhappy memories of their own schooling they will not be very willing to come into school. If you have already got to know parents before their child starts formal schooling, as we suggested in Chapter 4, you are more likely to be successful in maintaining that contact later. Instead of regarding 'invisible' parents as inadequate, we should try to understand how our education system has created that feeling of inadequacy. If we can build on the many skills that a parent already possesses she may realize that she may have something to offer to other children, too.

Many parents may be working at times when we arrange school meetings, or may have problems with baby-sitters. Do we organize our parental involvement schemes to suit only our school timetable without considering what might suit the parents? If parents do not have English as a first language, do we take the trouble to provide an interpreter? We need to show that we have books in school in the child's first language, and we need to persuade parents that they are welcome in the multi-racial classroom. It is important for a child to appreciate that his mother can read stories in his mother tongue not just to him, but to other children in his class. In one school the teachers are learning Indian dancing from one of the mothers in the lunch hour, and we know several mothers who enjoy teaching children to cook food from their country of origin. Whatever the reasons a parent may have for being unwilling to come into the classroom, we must be sure that we do not contribute our own lack of warmth. Our respect for a child's environment away from school is essential for that child's self-esteem and progress in the classroom. If we treat each child as an individual with needs and abilities we recognize as special, should we not also treat parents as individuals, and refrain from labelling them by social class or colour and making unsubstantiated assumptions about them. 'Invisible' parents may need a lot of encouragement to take part in school-based activities at first, because we have been blind to the possibilities of partnership.

Problems with colleagues

If you are convinced that you want to teach by sharing good books with children and parents, you must consider carefully how other members of staff view the issue. You may have difficulty in persuading colleagues who have not attended courses or done any research of the value of a new approach. These 'reluctant' colleagues yawn when you talk to them about Waterland's book, or tell them about the Share workshop you've just attended. 'Post-course euphoria' they sigh.

Post-course euphoria.

You need plenty of time to discuss the implications of inviting parents into school, and you will, generally speaking, need the support and enthusiasm of the headteacher. We do not underestimate the worries that may beset members of staff. You need to work together on the organization so that you are all sure how the scheme operates in your particular school. How are you going to keep records? What are you going to do about book supply? It will help if you attend INSET courses together, or ask someone from another school already working on a similar scheme to talk to you all after school. We have prepared a pack with books, research articles and a video, which schools in our area can borrow.

Those of us who were already working with parents on shared reading were available to talk to colleagues in other schools. Even if you take plenty of time for discussion, there may be still one member of staff who is reluctant, who remains unconvinced or unwilling to change time-honoured practice. We found that we were sometimes so enthusiastic that we rushed colleagues along too fast. There were occasions when the irresistible force met the immovable object. It is a good idea to try to arrange for an unwilling colleague to visit a school where shared reading is already established. It may be possible to let the teacher try a small pilot project with a group of children chosen by age rather than ability. There may be a trusted parent willing to come in to give the children extra time sharing a book. Most teachers are glad to have some of the burden of 'hearing reading' taken from their shoulders. If a teacher is unhappy to move away from the reading scheme, it is possible to let the children take 'real' books home and to keep the reading scheme for the classroom.

We do not think in the end that this is adequate because it gives children the message that reading for pleasure is not for the classroom! Teachers may be concerned that parents will express to them their worries about lack of structure and measured progress which they would not express to the head. It is only fair to show parents that you have a good record-keeping system, and teachers will feel more secure if they have a good monitoring system such as we outline in the chapter on assessment. The headteacher or literacy co-ordinator who is sympathetic to the feelings of colleagues will work out the best way to help reluctant colleagues to adjust to new ways of teaching reading.

If you are a class teacher interested in trying out shared reading, but have had no encouragement from the headteacher, who is apparently uninterested, you have to proceed by stealth. It is obvious that you cannot work with parents without the consent of the head. However, if you are an infant teacher, you will be meeting parents every day, so that you can build up a good relationship with them, in the hope that your head will become more sympathetic. In our survey of schools, we found only one male headteacher who was interested, and only one male teacher who attended our first two workshops which were attended by over 100 teachers representing 32 schools. We are glad to say that when word got round, more men began to take an interest. We began to wonder if reading was regarded as part of the woman teacher's domain like cooking and sewing! Overwhelming interest was shown by nursery and infant schools, with our female junior colleagues turning up in force too.

We suspect that upper junior teachers sometimes think that there is no more to be done once a child internalizes reading, and we often worry when we see children, who need a lot of practice and encouragement still, not getting the help they deserve in the junior classroom. If you have some leeway in your own classroom, but not much interest shown by your head, take heart! It will not be long before he becomes aware of the upsurge of interest in books from the children. If you already have a flourishing system operating, with books going home, and parents helping in school in the infant department, you have only to wait until the children move into the junior department. They will be far more articulate about books, they will be reading with confidence, and choosing books appropriate to their level of ability, and they will not hesitate to pester their new teacher to continue with bookbags. Maybe their parents will ask questions too. This is not the ideal way to introduce shared reading, but it has happened in some of our schools. Leading from the rear is better than doing nothing.

We have occasionally been challenged by politically aware colleagues who are not happy with the idea of non-professional help in school. This is a serious point and one which deserves careful consideration. It is easy to feel defensive, when we are working hard for the children we teach. Most teachers, particularly those in nursery and reception classes, are dismayed at the cuts in hours of welfare help. Many teachers feel that the needs of children have been ignored in cost-cutting exercises. In one school, parents offered to help for this very reason.

In an ideal world we would have the staffing to give every child the education he or she deserves. Even if we had the small classes we would like, and used falling rolls for the benefit of the children, we would still not have the time to devote to reading that home/school schemes provide. We believe that parental involvement in reading is based on sound educational theory, and is in no way an attempt to cover up cuts in spending, neither is it a response to political pressure for 'accountability'. We take the wider view that parents and teachers are, and always have been, partners in the child's education, and that it is our responsibility to make that partnership blossom for the benefit of the children in our care. When we asked parents how they saw their role in the classroom, they all made it plain that they wanted to be guided by the teacher, and reiterated the fact that they considered that the teacher was the professional and that they saw themselves as helpers in one area of the curriculum. As one parent said, 'The teacher is in charge, if the children want to sort out something, I always refer them to the teacher. That's her job, and I wouldn't dream of interfering.' This sounds as though the partnership is an unequal one, but the same parent and teacher confirmed that they saw each other as equal partners whose role changed depending on which one of them was in charge of the child. We hope that many of you will be able to develop equally trusting and supportive relationships with parents, and will work towards a united staff assured of the value of good home/school communication.

Books for parents

Bennett, J. (1985), *Learning to Read with Picture Books*. Thimble Press.
Bradman, T. (1986), *Will You Read Me a Story?* Thorsons Publishing.
Butler, D. (1982), *Babies Need Books*. Pelican.
Butler, D. (1986), *5 to 8*. Bodley Head.
Butler, D. and Clays, M. (1982), *Reading Begins at Home*. Heinemann.
Eccleshare, J. (1985), *Children's Books of the Year*. National Book League.
Meek, M. (1982), *Learning to Read*. Bodley Head.
Stevenage Literary Group, *Helping Your Child With Reading*. Available from Stevenage Teachers' Centre.
Trelease, J. (1986), *The Reading Aloud Handbook*. Penguin.
Waterland, L. (1985), *Read With Me*. Thimble Press.
Young, P. and Tyre, C. (1985), *Teach Your Child to Read*. Fontana.

CHAPTER 8

Positive repercussions

Shared reading in its broadest sense can be seen to have two strands:

1. that of involving parents;
2. that of using 'real books' for the teaching of reading.

Parental involvement may be in the home, as in the Haringey and Paired Reading approach, or within the classroom.

The practice of using 'real books', as advocated by Moon and Waterland, varies from school to school. Some schools have a completely free choice of books. Others grade their selections and/or incorporate reading scheme books in their book boxes. Alternatively, some schools retain reading scheme books as part of their language programme. The use of attractive and imaginative storybooks is having a great impact at the beginning stages of reading. Not only do they act as tremendous incentives to read, but give children more confidence and enthusiasm in this activity. Involving parents in this process, we suggest, has far more long-term repercussions within education.

Special needs

Every teacher who adopts shared reading sees it as an approach which benefits all children – i.e. no child and no parent is considered to be unsuitable. Topping first advocated Paired Reading for children with reading difficulties, and locally, this method is currently under consideration in some special schools and is also being instigated by our educational psychologists in mainstream schools. In some cases there are problems of illiteracy amongst the parents, and here we can learn from initiatives taken in inner-city areas, where these difficulties are on a much larger scale. In 1986 a Partners in Reading course was started in Leicester where a group of parents, some barely literate themselves, were shown how to help their children read. After two terms they had not only learned about reading, but had gained the confidence to approach their child's teacher and ask questions. They realized, too, that they were equipped to give their own children the help that they had never had. Shared reading in special schools is a whole new area now being examined by educational psychologists and specialist teachers. We need to concern ourselves with the needs of all children in our classroom, of whom 20 per cent could be classified as children with special needs.

One of the early signs of a child with special needs may be poor language skills – shown through unintelligible speech, limited vocabulary or lack or oral confidence or imagination. At the Coventry Community Education Development Centre, eight inner-city schools were evaluated on the language achievements of 881 five- to eleven-year-olds. Having involved parents over a period of 12 years, their test showed that these disadvantaged children, who would normally be expected to perform poorly on vocational tests, were able to match the performance of equivalent middle-class groups. Moreover their language development was considerably better than that of a national sample of the same socio-economic status.

The whole evaluation showed a high proportion of infants conversing confidently, using intelligible speech and a fairly wide vocabulary to a stranger. In writing, the junior children (over 90 per cent) could write legibly, fluently and accurately, and all age groups showed a positive attitude to reading. Peter Widlake, the centre's evaluation consultant, stated that 'such generally good achievements at many different age levels and in so many different aspects of language development cannot be dismissed as mere chance'. He maintained that the involvement of a large number of adults in schools was responsible for the stimulation and encouragement of the children. Some schools in our area are just beginning to recognize the valuable contribution adults can make in the areas of language development, and nursery and reception class teachers are asking volunteers to come in and help with the language development of some children.

There is no doubt that gifted children have every opportunity to progress rapidly, using the shared reading approach. The class teacher must ensure that these children are being fully extended in their reading material and are gradually incorporating more sophisticated reading strategies and skills. As their reading competence increases, so their written work should be reflecting their awareness of text and familiarity with such books as dictionaries and encyclopaedias. Results show too that readers in the middle ability range progress well, simply because of increased practice and exposure to books, and we would expect these children to be reading several months in advance of their chronological age.

However, it is with those children with reading difficulties that shared reading appears to be making most impact, and again it is with these children that parental involvement is seen to be most effective. In a parent involvement project in Sheffield (1982), carried out by Ashton, Stoney and Hannon, it was noted,

One of the most important factors in my opinion was the change brought about in parents who had despaired of their children doing well in reading. They were so keen to help their children improve and when even the slightest advance was made they noticed it and marvelled at it, which only encouraged the children more ... Those children who were so proficient and confident already did not seem to be very impressed with it, they were already used to reading at home. The others who were struggling and having difficulties gradually seemed to grow in confidence as the project continued. In general these children had avoided reading whenever possible. Their confidence seemed to spread into their other classwork.

Some of the parents of slow learners do not show any interest or support for their children's learning, and sadly it is such children who tend to drift through primary into secondary school with an increasing sense of failure.

In many schools, these children will receive attention from a remedial teacher, aiming to increase their competence in the basic skills. From our observations, the approach to reading tends to be heavily orientated towards phonics, often using a 'simple' reading scheme or 'reluctant reader' books. At the UKRA conference in London (1986) a Brent remedial teacher described the enthusiasm of such a 'failed' reader when she began to share his favourite sci-fi books with him. This boy made a dramatic improvement once he began to master the reading of these 'real' books and his remedial teacher now gives all her so-called failed readers the chance to start again, with a more positive approach. Not all results will be quite so dramatic and there is certainly a place for some precision monitoring for some children with specific reading difficulties. For example, children with poor visual memory will not progress very far without intervention. But in some cases there is evidence that precision monitoring, involving parents, is being introduced at an extremely early stage, without giving the child chance to succeed with a more relaxed approach first.

Into secondary school

Traditionally, children have always entered the secondary stage of education experiencing far less parental involvement. This has occurred for various reasons:

1. the child's gradual maturity fosters more independence;
2. the school may be some distance from the child's home;
3. as the child is introduced to more specialist subjects, the parent is less able to be in a position to help.

More recently, however, a number of initiatives have led to parents becoming aware of the functioning of the secondary sector – with such factors as more parent governors, projects linking school and industry or work experience schemes. In these instances, parents are being welcomed as partners for the mutual benefit of children, parents and teachers.

Children are suddenly faced with a multitude of new experiences on arrival at secondary school, and a recent survey (Open University 1987) indicated that books and materials they encounter are largely incomprehensible to them. Some schools are taking steps to rectify this situation either by a more careful monitoring of text used, or by operating their own systems of shared reading in order to maintain the children's reading skills. One year tutor has her own collection of stimulating books for her group, from which she encourages them to borrow. Other schools have timetabled library sessions for each child throughout the school, with plenty of informed staff available to discuss and recommend books. More schools now run flourishing regular family book evenings, when favourite books are reviewed and shared.

Attitudes

It is in this area that the most fundamental changes are being made, and where the most sensitive approaches are required. We hope that children's attitudes are gradually changing, especially as they move out of the infant school stage. Particularly as education becomes more investigative and assessment-based, we hope that they will begin to realize how much can be learned through discussion with an interested adult, be it teacher or parent. As teachers we need to look at our own prejudices and modify some of our earlier attitudes towards a partnership with parents. We need to come to terms and respect each other's role, and work out the best way of co-operating to benefit the children. Parents, too, are beginning to realize how crucial their support is for their child and, hopefully, can approach schools as informed supporters rather than confused critics, confident that their views will be listened to, and their contributions welcomed.

Other curriculum areas

Hearing their child read is an activity undertaken at some time by most parents, often at home and now increasingly in school. Today more schools are beginning to be aware of the many other skills parents may have to offer. The list, of course, is endless and covers every area of the curriculum, from the postman father describing his work to the nursery class to talented musicians, craftspeople, footballers, metalworkers or nuclear physicists! In one North Hertfordshire J.M.I. school we visited recently there was a proliferation of pottery made by the children to a very high standard. It transpired that a father was taking a local college-based course in this subject and it had been arranged that he could do his 12-week work experience in this school. Experience for him, certainly, but how beneficial for those fortunate 200 children. Individuals with such talents are not always quite so readily available, but experience is an ever present resource which can be tapped. A local secondary school used an office manager parent who set up the hall as a drawing office for the day. Here a group of business study pupils worked office hours on a real assignment, using imported equipment. This provided them with a real experience of functioning under working conditions.

'How do you spell genetic engineering?'

Improving the quality of reading has always been our aim, but there has been another bonus. We are finding that the quality of the children's writing is also improving. Because children are no longer limited to a basic vocabulary in their reading, they are exhibiting greater confidence in their early writing, showing a mature use of sentence structure, a willingness to experiment with spelling, and an understanding of the nature of 'story'. Children in the reception class are choosing to embark on whole stories, using their dictionaries much earlier than expected, and are able to sustain interest in a story written from day to day until they are satisfied with it. At the same time, a group of top infants have been competently using complicated sentence structures in writing about science experiments. Parents have also begun writing stories with their children, in a variety of languages, with their own excellent illustrations, making first reading books which can be used in school.

we stood   a Jam Jar Full of
water on the   table on a white
card Then we stood a piece of
cardBoord with two slits in it
hear the Jar we shone a Torch
on the slits so that two raysof
light shone onto The Jam Jar when
The rays of light went through the
Jam Jar they were bent and
when They came out the
other they
over this side They crossed
makes Things look bigger the glass
is how

Lois

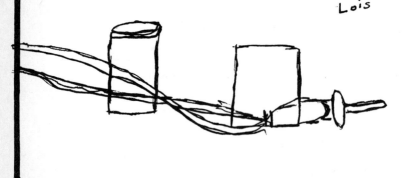

We made a projector with a light in a box. We put a magnifying glass on a stand in front of the light and then we made a screen and put it at the other end of the table. We put a slide in front of the lamp and showed it on the screen and it was upside down and it was very big. Then we put the slide down and the picture was the right way up.

Christopher

Two examples of six-year-olds free writing about science experiments.

Pre-school

Our observations show that good home/school liaison at the pre-school stage is invaluable. It benefits the child and its family, giving an awareness of what is expected from the child and providing practical guidelines and ideas to stimulate development. It benefits the school, because children are more likely to start their education from similar positions. In our experience much of this early home/school linkage exists, with communication established in a directed or sometimes spontaneous way. The most common home/school liaison occurs through the nursery class or, alternatively, the playgroup serving the school. Here the head or reception class teacher usually ensures a continuous collaboration between the two, and parents are encouraged to assist and be involved in many ways. Nurseries or playgroups that operate in the same buildings as their primary school have a tremendous advantage here, where pre-school experience must involve close contact with school.

We do feel, however, that home/school liaison could begin even earlier than this three- to four-year old stage. In many cases, this happens naturally when older siblings start school. But on visiting a local mothers and toddlers group recently, we found that its members mainly had children of pre-school age and had little awareness of the purposeful pre-school activities they could be involved in. There does seem to be a need for teachers to work in this area, visiting such groups and, even more necessary, contacting the more isolated mothers. Some sort of collaboration with health visitors by the education authorities could encourage more home-based stimulating activities for the pre-school child.

Ethnic minorities

This is an area in which gradually more and more initiatives are developing. In certain parts of Hertfordshire where the Asian communities are expanding, particularly in Watford, St Albans and North Hertfordshire, there are a number of successful home/school liaison schemes.

These have been promoted by classroom or E2L teachers, Language Centres or the County Multicultural Adviser. Whatever the scheme and whoever initiates it, the aims are common. Usually home/school liaison begins with reading, with the obvious objective that the child's reading will improve. With Shared Reading careful explanations are required. One North Hertfordshire school is planning to hold an evening, specifically for its 60 Asian families to introduce them to the practicalities of this method of reading together with their children. Explanatory letters in Punjabi will go home, an interpreter will be available on the evening and home visits will be offered to those unable to attend. The matter of home visiting is a very sensitive one, and great care must be taken so that it is not regarded as threatening or interventionalist. Certainly where home/school liaison is poor there is an argument in favour of home visiting to any family about which a teacher is concerned. Some areas could desperately do with some extra staffing to support this.

Having approached the parents to talk about learning to read initially, then we would hope for other positive outcomes. Our experience of a number of Asian families shows that although they may account for a large proportion of our school population, this is not represented by their attendance at open evenings, workshops, etc. We would hope that by more individual approaches, we may overcome their reluctance to come to school. Wendy Bloom evaluated a home visiting scheme in a multicultural middle school and made the following observations:

> A much better understanding was gained of individual children when seen in their home background with their family... Parents' concern was evident for their children's long-term prospects through education. There were many discussions about the balance that families were trying to maintain between the tensions of 'old' and 'new' ways of family and social life. Many of the young mothers felt isolated as they were not comfortable going out alone... It was felt in school that most Asian parents (fathers in particular) had a fairly formal and sometimes rather narrow view of learning... This, together with discussion, was starting to move these parents away from their sometimes rather rigid concept of what constitutes a learning activity.

Certainly we must show our Asian families that we do value their language and culture, and give them every opportunity to share parts of their heritage in school. We must reassure all our bi-lingual families that, particularly with shared reading the language that they use is immaterial; their children will benefit as much by discussing a book in their mother tongue as in English. Other parents may be persuaded to write or tape stories for their children in their community language.

Teacher/parent support groups

Parental involvement in school is part of a movement towards a community approach to child care and education. Not all areas have the motivation or the resources to approach this with the same commitment as say an area like Coventry, with its Community Education Policy. But there are indications of developments on a smaller scale in parts of Hertfordshire. St Albans Teacher's Centre, for example, recently held a day course on the Under 5s, open to teachers, nursery nurses, social workers and other interested parties.

We feel that we should initiate similar sessions, dealing with primary age children and include parents. There appear to be a number of courses, seminars, etc. on parental involvement, with few parents to be seen and heard! It is only when parents' views are expressed that true partnership can develop. A group of parents in Leicester, for example, were instrumental in starting up classes to deal with the problem of adult literacy. The introduction of shared reading often does lead to the identification of illiterate parents and may well lead on to extra provision for them by the sensitive school. More collaboration between parents and teachers can involve joint meetings and mutual support groups. Accompanying this we have observed more inter-school activity. As part of their own staff development, teachers are increasingly visiting other local schools to observe a variety of recent developments in classroom practice, among them parental involvement and shared reading. This more open approach and the willingness of so many teachers to share their ideas can only be beneficial to our schools and the children we teach.

As clusters of schools developing shared reading evolve all over the country, it is interesting to hear of more inter-authority initiatives. We are embarking on a combined Northamptonshire/Hertfordshire project on writing, involving joint day courses and shared teacher/adviser expertise. We have also established a link with the London Borough of Merton, involving workshops and visits by inspectors, headteachers and teachers, each looking at the other authority's approach to reading.

Probationary teachers

Atkin and Bastiani (1985) paint a gloomy picture of student teacher preparation for parental contact. They surveyed 96 teacher training establishments and discovered that one-third of primary and one-half of secondary students received no training in this vital area of school life. It now appears that the situation will worsen, since stipulations of the 1986 Education Act give colleges even less opportunity to introduce this subject to students, because of imposition of other educational priorities. Therefore it is absolutely vital that probationary teachers receive guidance in their written and verbal communication with parents. It is extremely difficult, for example, for young, inexperienced teacher to feel confident enough to open up their classrooms to parents. They need to be given time and space to develop their classroom management techniques and provided with ample opportunity to observe other more experienced teachers practising parental involvement.

CHAPTER 9

Conclusions

No one will dispute that enthusiastic teachers will generate enthusiastic pupils and that, whatever the subject may be, success is more likely. For this reason we are not presenting this approach to reading as being necessarily the most successful for every teacher. Other methods as described in similar books will achieve similar results when used exclusively or alongside shared reading. We have observed, however, important plus factors which would lead us to recommend strongly consideration of shared reading.

- Our children have developed the same confident approach to writing as they show towards reading. Early writing is no longer restricted to simple sentences, using simple vocabulary. Having been exposed to a wide vocabulary in their reading they are using quite complex sentence structures as they write, and soon believe they can write whole stories.

- Many parents too are exhibiting a new confidence in their support of their children and in their interest in classroom learning. We are just beginning to initiate shared writing projects which can develop positive links between home and school.

- Teachers are finding a new confidence in partnering parents. In the current climate of educational reform, they are discovering the benefits of the staunch support to be gained from informed parents, when decisions have to be made which could be crucial in terms of children's educational needs.

- Children come to have a real enjoyment of books, and an appreciation of favourite authors and different types of text and illustration. They develop critical faculties, and read a wide range of story, poetry and information books. By promoting shared reading right through the primary school and beyond we hope that we are encouraging a generation of life-long readers, who will always regard books as a constant source of pleasure and information.

References

Anderson, E. (1983), 'Cohesion in the classroom' in *Australian Journal of Reading*, Vol. 6. No. 1. 35–42.

Anderson, E. (1984), 'Reading and the bilingual child' in Miller, N. (ed.), *Bilingualism and Language Disability*. London. Croom Helm. 154–166.

Applebee, A.N. (1978), *The Child's Concept of Story*. London. The University of Chicago Press.

Ashton, C.J., Stoney, A.H. and Hannon, P.W. (1986), *A Reading at Home Project in a First School*. Support for Learning. Vol. 1. No. 1.

Atkin, J. and Bastiani, J. (1985), *Preparing Teachers to Work With Parents*. University of Nottingham.

Bastiani, J. (ed.) (1978), *Written Communication Between Home and the School*. University of Nottingham. School of Education.

Bissex, G. (1980), Gnys at Wrk. Cambridge, Mass. Harvard University Press.

Blank, M., Rose, S.A. and Berlin, L.J. (1978), *The Language of Learning – The Pre-School Years*. New York. Grune & Stratton.

Bloom, W. (1987), *Partnership With Parents in Reading*. Sevenoaks. Hodder & Stoughton.

Bradman, T. (1986), *Will You Read Me a Story?* Wellingborough. Thorsons Publishing Group.

Brown, R. and Bellugi, U. (1964), 'Three processes in the child's acquisition of syntax' in *Harvard Educational Review*, Vol. 34. No. 2. 133–151.

Butler, D. (1982), *Babies Need Books*. London. Pelican.

Cazden, C.B. (1983), 'Play with language and metalinguistic awareness' in Donaldson *et al.* (eds), *Early Childhood Development and Education*. Oxford. Blackwell. 302–307. First published in *Urban Review* (1974), Vol. 7. No. 1.

Central Advisory Council for Education (1967), *Children and their Primary Schools*. (Plowden Report). London, HMSO.

Chapman, L.J. (1987), *Reading: From 5–11 Years*. Milton Keynes. Open University Press.

Clark, M.M. (1976), *Young Fluent Readers*, London. Heinemann.

Clay, M.M. (1972), *Reading: the Patterning of Complex Behaviour*. London. Heinemann.

Community Education Development Centre, Coventry. Ed. John Rennie. Various pamphlets.

Daniels, J.C. and Diack, H. (1974), *The Standard Reading Test*. London. Chatto & Windus.

Davies, F. and Greene, T. (1984), *Reading for Learning in the Sciences*, Edinburgh. Oliver & Boyd.

DES (1975), *A Language for Life* (Bullock Report). London, HMSO.

DES (1977), *A New Partnership For Our Schools* (Taylor Report). London, HMSO.

DES (1985), *Better Schools*. London, HMSO.

DES (Assessment of Performance Unit) (1979), *Primary Survey 1*, London, HMSO.

DES (Assessment of Performance Unit) (1980), *Primary survey 2*, London, HMSO.

Donaldson, M. (1978), *Children's Minds*. Glasgow. Collins/Fontana.

Donaldson, M., Grieve, R. and Pratt, C. (eds) (1983), *Early Childhood Development and Education*. Oxford. Blackwell.

Douglas J. (1964), *The Home and the School*. London. MacGibbon and Kee Ltd.

Ferreiro, E. (1985), 'The relationship between oral and written language: The children's viewpoints' in Clark, M.M. (ed.), *New Directions in the Study of Reading*. London. The Falmer Press. 83–94.

Goodman, Y. (1984), 'Initial literacy' in Goelman, H., Oberg, A. and Smith, F. (eds), *Awakening to Literacy*. London. Heinemann.

Halliday, M.A.K. (1975), *Learning How to Mean*. London. Edward Arnold.

Hunter-Grundin, E. and Hunter-Grundin, H. (1980), *Literacy Profiles*. Test Agency.

Jackson, A. and Hannon, P. (1981), The Belfield Reading Project. Belfield Community Council.

Lunzer, E.A. and Gardner, K. (eds) (1979), *The Effective Use of Reading*. London. Heinemann Educational Books.

Midwinter, E. (1972), *Projections: An Educational Priority Area at Work*. London. Ward Lock Educational.

Moon, C. (1977), *Individualised Reading*. University of Reading.

Moseley, C. and Moseley, D. (1977), *Language and Reading among Underachievers*. Windsor. NFER Nelson.

Neale, M.D. (1966 2nd ed), *Neale Analysis of Reading Ability*. London. Macmillan.

Paley, V.G. (1981), *Wally's Stories*. Cambridge, Mass. Harvard University Press.

Pritchard, D. and Rennie, J. (1978), *Reading Involving Parents*. Coventry Education Committee.

Smidt, S. (1986), *Language Matters*, ILEA.

Steffensen, M.S. (1981), Register, Cohesion and Cross-cultural Reading Comprehension. Technical Report No. 220. Center for the Study of Reading, University of Illinois at Urbana-Champaign.

Swinson, J.M. (1986), 'Paired reading: a critique' in *Support for Learning*, Vol. 1. No. 2. 29–32.

Templin, M.C. (1957), 'Certain language skills in children' in *Institute of Child Welfare Monograph*, 26. Minneapolis. University of Minnesota Press.

Tizard, B., Mortimore, J. and Burchall, B. (1980), *Involving Parents in Infant and Nursery Schools*. Oxford, Blackwell.

Tizard B., Mortimore J. and Burchell, B. (1981), *School, Sweet School. Involving Parents in Nursery and Infant Schools*. Grant McIntyre.

Tizard, J., Schofield, W. and Hewison, J. (1982), 'Collaboration between teachers and parents in assisting children's reading', in *British Journal of Educational Psychology*, Vol. 52. No. 1.

Topping, K. and McKnight, G. (1984), Paired Reading and Parent Power. Special Education Forward Trends. Vol. 11.

Topping, K. and Wolfendale, S. (eds) (1985), *Parental Involvement in Children's Reading*. London. Croom Helm.

Trevarthen, C. (1974), 'Conversations with a two-month-old' in *New Scientist*, Vol. 62. 230–233.

Waterland, L. (1986), *Read With Me*. Stroud, Glos. The Thimble Press.

Weir, R. (1962), *Language in the Crib*. The Hague. Mouton.

Wells, G. (1982), Language, Learning and Education. Centre for the Study of Language and Communication. University of Bristol.

Wood, A. (1974), Parents and the Curriculum. Unpublished thesis University of Southampton.

Young, D. (1969), *Group Reading Test*. University of London Press.

Young, P. and Tyre, C. (1986), *Teach Your Child to Read*. London. Fontana.

Index